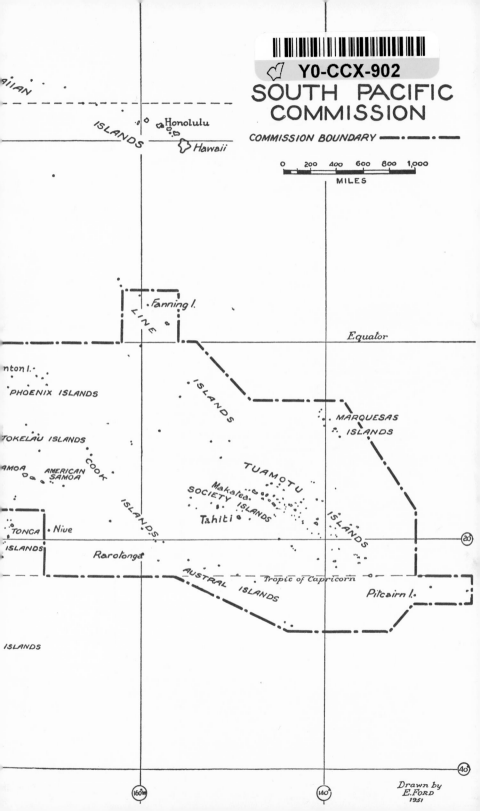

SOUTH PACIFIC
COMMISSION

COMMISSION BOUNDARY ▬ ▪ ▬ ▪ ▬

0   200   400   600   800   1,000

MILES

Hawaiian ISLANDS

Honolulu

Hawaii

LINE

Fanning I.

Equator

Canton I.

PHOENIX ISLANDS

ISLANDS

TOKELAU ISLANDS

MARQUESAS
ISLANDS

Samoa

AMERICAN
SAMOA

COOK

TUAMOTU

Makatea

SOCIETY
ISLANDS

TONGA   Niue

Tahiti

ISLANDS

ISLANDS

Rarotonga

(20)

AUSTRAL ISLANDS

Tropic of Capricorn

Pitcairn I.

ISLANDS

(40)

160°   140°

*Drawn by
E. Ford
1951*

SOCIAL ANTHROPOLOGY IN MELANESIA

SOCIAL ANTHROPOLOGY IN MELANESIA

A Review of Research

A. P. ELKIN

M.A., SYDNEY, PH.D., LONDON

*Professor of Anthropology
in the University of Sydney*

*Published under the auspices of the
South Pacific Commission*

GREENWOOD PRESS, PUBLISHERS
WESTPORT, CONNECTICUT

Library of Congress Cataloging in Publication Data
Elkin, Adolphus Peter, 1891-
    Social anthropology in Melanesia.

    Reprint of the 1953 ed. published by Oxford University
Press, London, New York.
    Includes bibliographies and index.
    1. Ethnology--Melanesia. 2. Anthropological research
--Melanesia. I. Title.
GN668.E44 1976   993   76-11834
ISBN 0-8371-8933-0

First published in 1953 by Oxford Unviersity Press, London,
New York under the auspices of the South Pacific Commission

Reprinted with the permission of South Pacific Commission

Reprinted in 1976 by Greenwood Press,
a division of Williamhouse-Regency Inc.

Library of Congress Catalog Card Number 76-11834

ISBN 0-8371-8933-0

Printed in the United States of America

The South Pacific Commission is an advisory and consultative body set up by the six Governments responsible for the administration of island territories in the South Pacific region. Its purpose is to recommend to the Member Governments means for promoting the well-being of the peoples of these territories. It is concerned with social, economic and health matters. Its headquarters are at Noumea, New Caledonia.

The Commission was established by an Agreement between the Governments of Australia, France, the Netherlands, New Zealand, the United Kingdom, and the United States of America, signed at Canberra on 6th February, 1947, and finally ratified on 29th July, 1948. Until 7th November, 1951, the area of the Commission's activities comprised territories lying generally south of the Equator from and including Netherlands New Guinea in the west to the French Establishments in Oceania and Pitcairn in the east. On 7th November, 1951, an additional Agreement was signed at Commission headquarters in Noumea on behalf of the six participating Governments, extending the scope of the Commission to include Guam and the Trust Territory of the Pacific Islands under United States Administration.

The Commission consists of twelve Commissioners, two from each Government, and meets twice a year. The first Session was held in May 1948. There are two auxiliary bodies, the Research Council and the South Pacific Conference.

The Research Council, which assembles once a year, held its first meeting in May 1949. Members are appointed by the Commission, and are selected for their special knowledge of the questions with which the Commission is concerned, and the problems of the territories in these fields. The chief function of the Research Council is to advise the Commission what investigations are necessary. Arrangements to carry out those that are approved are the responsibility of the Secretary-General and other principal officers.

The South Pacific Conference, which meets at intervals not exceeding three years, consists of delegates from the local inhabitants of the territories, who may be accompanied by advisers. The first Conference was held in Suva in April 1950, and was attended by delegates from the fifteen territories and from the Kingdom of Tonga.

CONTENTS

INTRODUCTION

THIS survey and plan of research in social anthropology has been prepared at the invitation of the South Pacific Commission. Most, if not all, of the relevant literature has been examined. I also discussed the practical problems on which research might well throw light with administrative officers and with missionaries from many parts of the region, from Netherlands New Guinea to the New Hebrides, whenever opportunity offered. In addition, thanks to the Commission, I recently spent four and a half weeks in New Guinea, discussing problems for research with persons in close touch with native affairs, obtaining facts and figures, and visiting parts of the Territories with which I was not familiar, in particular the thickly populated Central Highlands. Here alone are half a million or more people. I thank the Administrator and members of his administration for very real and ready help.

As a result of my visits to Papua and New Guinea and of my close association with these Territories since 1933 as Professor of Anthropology, University of Sydney, and Chairman of the Anthropological Committee of the Australian National Research Council, I am more familiar personally with administration and missionary activity in them, than elsewhere in the region. To do this task as thoroughly as I would wish, I should have spent several weeks in the other Territories also. However, Papua and New Guinea contain well over a million people, probably more than two-thirds of the total population of the whole region. As for the rest, both the survey and recommendations have been well based.

The method has been (1) to evaluate the different types of information and research results which are available; (2) to survey the whole region showing our present knowledge, indicating significant gaps, and suggesting problems and projects; and (3) to provide principles and a plan of research with projects classified accordingly. The lists of projects which are recommended as the most important and immediately necessary in the area are to be found in the five sub-sections under "Classification of Research Projects" in Part III.

Our great need in the present phase of anthropological research is co-ordination and co-operation between all authorities and individuals concerned, in a plan which will throw light on the dark places which beset administration and all welfare agencies in New Guinea–Melanesia. In addition, we need from field-workers both linguistic efficiency and anthropological expertness, and also willingness to devote up to four or even five years in the case of some of the projects. These and related matters are elaborated in the Report.

The suggested plan naturally deals with individual projects, each of which would be pursued amongst a particular people by a field-worker (singly or in co-operation with others) for a period varying according to the nature of the project. Such field-workers will be temporarily engaged in their particular projects for anything from say one to five years. Some may be fairly recently trained, and will be under direction, while others, we hope, will be well experienced, seconded for the time being from senior positions.

Some of the projects recommended in this Report, however, and others which will arise as problems from time to time, could be carried out by anthropologists permanently appointed to research positions in the New Guinea–Melanesia region. In the body of the Report I have urged the appointment by some missionary societies of mission anthropologists to help them in their approach, in their difficulties, and to evaluate functionally the effects of their activities.

I have also referred to government anthropologists, but have not stressed the matter, because the Administration—Papua and New Guinea—with the largest area of responsibility, plans to appoint two at once. If any of the other administrations would take a similar step, it would be all to the good. Netherlands New Guinea certainly provides the opportunity for one such life-long appointment.

In addition to government and mission anthropologists there is a third possibility: the South Pacific Commission itself should consider appointing an all-round, well experienced social anthropologist as a permanent member of its research staff, to work mainly on short-term projects. These could be of several types. They could be related to the Commission's own plans of inquiry and development by providing the fundamental sociological basis for implementing projects in the fields of agriculture, medicine, hygiene, education, economics and others. The human element in all such schemes is ultimately basic, and it must be understood so that co-operation be gained.

Further, the Commission's own anthropologist could be made available at the request of, or with the consent of, any administration to work on a project or problem in that administration's territory.

This would, indeed, be real co-operation. It would be especially valuable in those territories which do not possess their own anthropologists, but even in those which do, the additional help would be much appreciated.

In particular, such an anthropologist, fully conversant with all relevant literature, and experienced in observing the behaviour of native peoples and in making contact with them, will be able to carry out those social science inquiries of the survey type, in which both the Commission and administrations are particularly interested. These include principles and methods of native political organizations; land ownership; exchange and trading relationships; marriage and "separation", and "socialization" of the personality. In most cases, however, especially those in which he hasn't sufficient time to follow out the ramifications of the institution being surveyed, his reports will need checking by intensive work because of the inter-relationship of the different aspects of the culture and of the social structure.

I strongly recommend to the Commission such an appointment. I realize that a similar appointment might be made also from other fields of social science; but if there can only be one, I suggest that he be a social anthropologist, for as such, he should have a good understanding of social psychology, of language, and of the function of economic, political and other aspects of community life and endeavour in the total pattern.

Finally, I thank the Commission for entrusting this task to me, Mr. H E. Maude for his personal interest in its performance, Miss Barbara Glaser for indexing the material from German Journals, Dr. A. Capell for assisting with Dutch literature and in other ways, Miss Joyce Williams for helping in library search, and Miss Barbara Smith for typing—and typing. The last three are members of my own Department.

The University of Sydney,
August 7, 1950.   A. P. ELKIN.

NOTE

THIS report was completed and presented to the South Pacific Commission in August 1950. Since then, several of the suggested projects have been undertaken or planned. The study of change in the Trobriands has been made. Professor Firth returned to Tikopia and Dr. Fortune to the Kamamentina headwaters in the Bena-Bena region. Dr. Mead has planned to return to Manus in 1953. First "terms" of research have been carried out, and second "terms" begun, in the Madang, Garoka and Kainantu regions. A study of the Orokaiva today, begun towards the end of 1950, was cut short by the tragic eruption of Mt. Lamington. A valuable project, emphasizing economic re-adjustment, has been carried out in south-west Papua, and M. Guiart has continued his research in the New Hebrides. Such facts as these, together with the titles of recent publications, have been added to the text, which otherwise remains as when first presented.

I would, however, emphasize one point. My examination of the literature has made me realize that our knowledge of the Papuans and Melanesians in most of the total region lacks depth. We can describe social structure, economic activities, magical forms and some myths. Here and there too, the language has been analysed, and a few attempts have been made to formulate personality types. But we have not learnt the system of values and of attitudes, nor the philosophy and religion of the peoples studied. Investigators do not seem to have been admitted into, or to have grasped, the meaning of life as held by Papuans and Melanesians. This is not surprising. Administrators, missionaries, employers and anthropologists have been comparatively few in number, and, to the native peoples, have been intruders. It was no very difficult matter for these peoples to work out methods of intellectual and external adaptation which satisfied the European and at the same time protected the fundamental aspects of native culture, philosophy and social structure. Administrators had no time to penetrate this screen; employers were not interested; missionaries sometimes thought they had done so, or else waited for change in the rising generations; and anthropologists, in spite of their careful descriptions and inferences, were just as innocent.

What else could be expected from the last group? Six to twelve months' research will enable certain selected series of observations to be made. But he who thinks that he can master a Papuan or even a Melanesian language and culture in such a period, and understand a people's "way of life and thought", not just the aspects of it which they manifest to him, is deluding himself. Of course no experienced anthropologist thinks like this. In the past he has aimed at lesser, though still important goals; and with so much ground, so many peoples to be surveyed, we had to be satisfied.

Now, however, while such short-term sampling still has value, and is all that many individual workers can afford to do, we need, where possible, that longer and deeper research which leads to understanding. It means the devotion of five or six years to a project, but it would provide satisfaction for the anthropologist and valuable knowledge for the administrator and missionary. I believe, too, that since the war the native peoples of the region will co-operate in such intensive research in a way they would not have contemplated in pre-war years. I therefore draw particular attention to Part III of this Report, in which this matter is discussed.

November 10, 1952   A. P. ELKIN

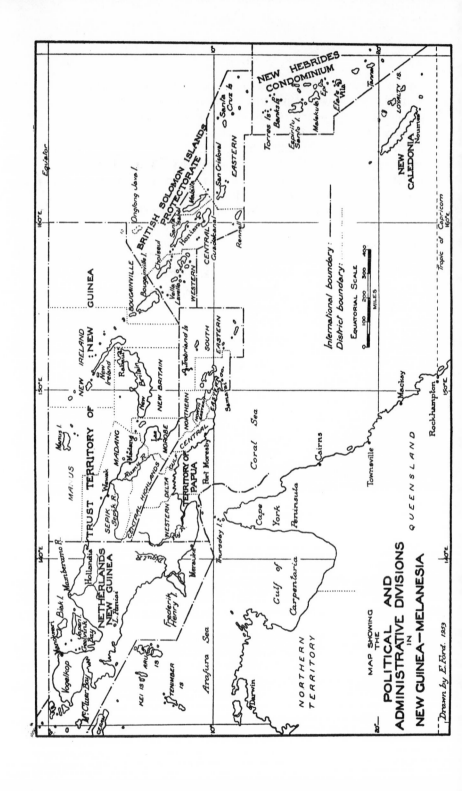

MAP SHOWING
THE
POLITICAL AND
ADMINISTRATIVE DIVISIONS
IN
NEW GUINEA—MELANESIA

Drawn by E. Ford. 1953

PART I

TYPES OF ETHNOGRAPHICAL RECORD AND RESEARCH
UP TO 1950

EXPLORERS AND TRAVELLERS

KNOWLEDGE of the native peoples of these island regions has been obtained by three groups of persons, the results varying in both scientific and practical value.

The first consists of explorers' and travellers' observations of what they see and the little they learn through inadequate interpreting facilities; such observers are also handicapped by having no plan or only a very inadequate plan of observation and inquiry,—that is they do not grasp the significance of social structure, social organization and culture, and the way in which institutions are interrelated and function. Moreover, their sojourn in any area is brief. In earlier days, however, and in new areas in more recent years, such exploring, when conducted by an experienced administrative officer, has usually prepared the way for the steady and peaceful advance of government control. The exploring contact has revealed (1) locations and a rough idea of numbers in "new" groups or tribes; (2) the latter's basic economic interests—that is whether gardening or foodgathering, or both, and if gardening, the type of crops and the methods used; the media of exchange or barter; housing; and living conditions generally; (3) some indication of magic and religion, if tabu signs, ceremonial posts, houses or platforms, or burial paraphernalia were in evidence; and (4) some awareness, not necessarily reliable, of the temperament of the newly discovered people: for example, whether they were warlike, resentful of strangers, interested in new phenomena or afraid of such, and likely to welcome, tolerate or resist administrative control and the intrusion of missionaries and settlers.

This explanatory work has been essential. The records may be read in the reports of patrol officers, and in more popular form in books which some of them have written. These reports also contain geographical information about the country and routes traversed. Indeed, the work is fundamentally geographical, rather than anthropological, for the explorer can do little more than describe the peoples he finds, as part of the geographical setting. But it is basic to later study of those peoples.

Books by administrative officers (recording their explorations and/or incidents in their work) include:

W. N. Beaver, *Unexplored New Guinea*, 1920.

C. A. W. Monckton, *Some Experiences of a New Guinea Magistrate*, Two series, 1920.

W. R. Humphries, *Patrolling in Papua*, 1923.

J. G. Hides, *Through Wildest Papua*, 1935. Idem. *Papuan Wonderland*, 1936.

I. F. Champion, *Across New Guinea from the Fly to the Sepik*, 1932.

J. H. P. Murray, *Papua or British New Guinea*, 1912, and *Papua of To-day*, 1925.

Sir Hubert Murray's are included because they contain records of explorations by members of the staff, and also accounts of, and reflections on, administrative problems.

Quite distinct from, and of less practical value than, these truly geographical and exploratory accounts, are the popular articles and books written by later fleeting visitors, no matter how much they have collected by interviewing officials, missionaries and settlers and by talking to a few natives through interpreters or in a poor pidgin. These might well be interesting and very readable travelogues, with plenty of reliable information; but the central point is the traveller and writer, not the native society and culture, not the interaction of native and non-native in the process of culture-contact and of the contact and clash of men and women of different skins and attitude. The information is piecemeal and out of context and therefore of little value for science or for the promotion of native welfare.

The provision of handbooks which were designed for travellers and other persons in contact with native peoples, such as *Notes and Queries*, six editions of which have been issued by the Royal Anthropological Institute of Great Britain and Ireland, the early set of questions drawn up by James G. Frazer, *Fragment d'un plan de sociologie déscriptive* by Marcel Mauss, and his later *Manuel d'Ethnographie* designed for the same purpose, are too long and tedious for such observers; indeed, the later editions and issues are really introductory handbooks, and need to be accompanied by some anthropological training if the results are really to be satisfactory.

There is, however, a sub-group of travellers, which does make a useful anthropological contribution, providing some information where otherwise nothing would be known, and also indicating useful

places for research. These people are or have been for the most part
natural historians or surgeons. They tend to give actual examples of
cultural behaviour, and not merely to describe such behaviour in
general terms. This enhances the value of their contribution. Some of
them tackle the obvious problem of depopulation, and so provide
useful facts and a record of opinions as to causes.

Amongst these are: H. B. Guppy, M.A., *The Solomon Islands and
Their Natives*, 1887; Emil Stephan, surgeon, *Neu-Mecklenburg: Die
Küste von Umuddu bis Kap St. Georg*, 1907, (based on a visit to the area
in 1904, and written in collaboration with F. Graebner, the celebrated
ethnologist); Fritz Sarasin, a naturalist, *Neu-Caledonien und die
Loyalty-Inseln*, 1917, (based on a visit in 1911-12); J. R. Baker, zoolo-
gist, *Man and Animals in the New Hebrides*, 1929, (expeditions in 1922-23
and 1927); Tom Harrisson, biologist, *Savage Civilization*, 1937, (based
on two years, 1934-35, in the New Hebrides—very valuable for
anthropology).

2

MISSIONARIES, ADMINISTRATORS AND SETTLERS

THE second type of observer-recorder is the person whose work lies in the midst of, and in varying degrees with, a native people, and who cannot help gaining over a period of years some knowledge of the latter, even though it be very superficial; indeed, in most cases they must do so, if they are to make any headway in their own sphere of activity. This type includes the missionary, the administrative officer in his district work, and the non-native settler.

Missionaries

Of these, the missionary has had the best opportunity and the most success in obtaining a knowledge of the community amongst whom he was or is working. In New Guinea-Melanesia, there has usually been at least one member of the staff in a district with a good or reasonably good education, and in some cases with ability and training in linguistics. Moreover, missionaries generally remain for a number of years, perhaps for many years, in the same district. Consequently, through their growing familiarity with the language, their work of translating the Bible and forms of Service, and their efforts to alter the native standards of behaviour, they have the opportunity to learn much about natives, in particular about certain individuals and about certain customs.

As a result, missionaries have made many useful contributions to the anthropology of parts of the region. Unfortunately, however, only a few missionaries have had any anthropological training, or more than a very short introductory and over-loaded course in the subject. Moreover, they are usually very busy with many tasks in addition to what should be the two basic ones, learning and improving in the language and understanding the society and culture; basic because the culture makes the native people, as individuals and as a group, what they are.

Consequently, missionaries have not provided such rounded studies of the society and culture, with its structure, pattern and institutions, which are required by science and are, therefore, at the same time, of practical value for wise and sound missionary activity; for this latter is a potent factor of culture-change, and may also cause change in the social structure, an even more serious matter.

There are still missionaries who say that anthropology is concerned with recording a people's customs, and that if they had time they would help. They seem to have in mind the old-fashioned type of "List of Questions", and fail to see that anthropology is concerned with something which they ought themselves to grasp: namely, that the society and culture to which the natives of their area belong, is a functioning complex of institutions, customs, sanctions, beliefs, rituals and forms of activity, correlated with a definite social structure, and forming as a whole a process through time. Further, it is with this complex of a succession of human beings through the generations, and their changing cultural heritage through time, that they, the missionaries, like the administrators, and to some extent the settlers, are concerned:—modifying, undermining, or even destroying it—either intentionally or unintentionally.

It is this failure to see clearly the implications and needs of their own work which explains, for the most part, the inadequacy, for both scientific and practical purposes, of most of the missionaries' contributions to anthropology. It is also an explanation of the fact that much missionary work remains on the surface of native life. Very often, apart from a few individual natives, the fundamental beliefs and sanctions remain what they were; the old-time rites are secretly retained in practice or in memory, to be reviewed when opportunity occurs, or to form the core of Cargo Cults in time of psychological stress.

Contributions by Missionaries

The simple fact is that, in spite of many useful articles on some aspects of native culture, mostly some customs and beliefs, missionaries have not provided those basic studies and books which are urgently needed in this period of rapid change and keen desire. Possibly one of the best missionary anthropologist books produced was Junod's *Life of a South African Tribe*, in two volumes. The very title, especially the words "life" and "tribe", is significant. Not customs as such, but the life of the community as a whole, with its structure and culture, was the theme; and each section ended with an application of its content to practical mission problems.

Only two or three works by missionaries in the New Guinea-Melanesia regions approach this standard. Examples are, the *Waropen*, 1947, by Dr. Held, which was the result of field research in a living society and culture by a trained anthropologist who was at the time connected with a mission society; he now holds a Professorial Chair in Djakarta; *Notes d'Ethnologie Néo-Caledonienne*, 1930, and *Documents Néo-Caledoniens*, 1930, *Vocabulaire et Grammaire de la langue Houailou*, 1935, by M. Leenhardt, formerly a missionary in New Caledonia; and *In Unknown New Guinea*, 1926, by W. J. V. Saville (who was guided by B. Malinowski).

Codrington's *Melanesians*, however, with all its merits and flashes of insight, does not give us a picture of any functioning community in such a way that we see any principles of cohesion or change. Likewise, the Rev. Dr. W. G. Ivens' big book, *Melanesians of the South-east Solomon Islands*, fails, although he tried to make his "quest of customs" cover as far as possible the whole life of the people, so that it should be of value "as a record of a state of things that is fast passing away" (from the Preface.) We are grateful for this book, for the same writer's *Island Builders of the Pacific* and, amongst others, for Dr. Codrington's book, the Rev. George Brown's *Melanesians and Polynesians*, the Rev. A. Kleintitschen's *Die Kustenbewohner der Gazelle-Halbinsel*, 1906, the Rev. J. Guis' *La Vie des Papous*, 1936, (but written in 1897-1901); the missionaries: S. Lehner, Stolz, G. Bamier, H. Zahn and C. Keysser who wrote Volume III of R. Neuhauss's *Deutsch-Neu-Guinea*, 1911, and the many articles on the region by learned missionaries in *Anthropos*. Moreover, these types of contributions *should be encouraged* by all anthropological journals and by publishers.

The establishment of an international anthropological journal, *Anthropos*, by a missionary order, the Society of the Divine Word, and its maintenance for the past forty-five years has itself been a remarkable contribution to anthropology, and the foundation more recently (in 1937) of a similar journal, the *Annali Lateranensi*, by the *Pontificio Museo* is also very welcome. Through these media, the anthropological and linguistic studies of Roman Catholic missionaries are made available to the scientific world. Moreover, *Anthropos* has published articles by anthropologists who are not affiliated with the Roman Catholic Church.

Such publications imply that the missionary orders of this Church expect at least some of its members to be capable of contributing articles acceptable on an international standard. This means that training in anthropology and linguistics is provided for its missionaries.

The New Guinea-Melanesian region has benefited from this policy. Their linguistic contributions have been of great value, and while many of the anthropological articles have been limited to the description of particular customs and beliefs, or in some cases, to writing in the light of Dr. W. Schmidt's theories, the recent and present tendency is for more complete studies, and towards the use of the functional method in analysis and description. Dr. Georg Höltker, Society of the Divine Word, and editor of *Anthropos*, who himself worked for a period in New Guinea, is encouraging this tendency. Amongst the best of the present writers in this group are A. Aufinger, A. Schaeffer, C. Laufer, P. H. Meyer, J. Blaes and J. Nilles.[1]

All this is to the good, and we hope that anthropological research (and the present tendency with regard to problems) will be continued not only by this group, but also by others.

The fact is, we need from missionaries work done along the lines of Dr. H. I. Hogbin's *Experiments in Civilization*, in which we see the past and present, and in which we are presented with an analysis of changes which are in progress, and with methods for consideration. We need from the missions some books like F. E. Williams' *Orokaiva Society*, a sound anthropological, and yet very human, study of the Orokaiva, or his *Drama of Orokolo*, which at least reveals the serious gap in life made by the dying out of a remarkable institution which had many ramifications. Whiting's *Becoming a Kwoma*, or M. Mead's *Growing up in New Guinea* are examples of another kind of study which is needed, if our plans for native education are to be sound.

Mission Anthropologists

True, these are by trained and full time anthropologists, and missionaries may rightly answer that they have not the time and very seldom the training to make these sorts of investigations. This is most unfortunate, for leading missionaries by reason of their continued residence in one field, and their acquaintance with native languages, are in a key position. They could provide that basis of knowledge which is required for the introduction of those changes in native peoples'

[1]Fr. J. Nilles holds the Diploma of Anthropology from the University of Sydney. His thesis has been published in *Oceania*, September 1950, under the title: *The Kuman of the Chimbu region, Central Highlands, New Guinea.*—A.P.E., November, 1952.

mental outlook, beliefs and skills, and in their relationship to the outside world, on which their progress depends. It would seem most desirable that in a few selected fields in the New Guinea-Melanesian regions, each of the main mission societies appoint a well-trained field anthropologist to its staff. Such a person, of course, would be completely in sympathy with the Christian aims of the mission, but their work for the mission would be only in a very small degree evangelism, teaching or healing. Their task would be a specialist one, the complete study of a selected sample community in the mission area, or of special problems.

The approach must be functional and sociological, seeing the community and its culture as a whole and as a process, so that the significance of present activity for the future can be determined. The anthropologist should be basic to missionary methods. In addition to concentrating on a selected community for a few years, he would be available to study and report on happenings anywhere in the mission's field, when this seemed necessary.

Missions might feel that they cannot afford this essential member of staff—who will be termed by many a luxury. My own experience over twenty and more years (and that of anthropological colleagues who are quite sympathetic to missions) is that the position is so important at this stage of native development that the governments concerned should subsidize missions for this purpose; provided, of course, that the person appointed is a thoroughly qualified anthropologist of the calibre to whom a University or Research Council would award a Fellowship for field-work.

As so much responsibility for native development is of necessity in the hands of missions, this type of co-operation should appeal to governments and also to mission authorities. Such appointments are, of course, parallel to those of government anthropologists, whose value has been proved. In some political regions, both government and mission anthropologists might well be appointed; in others, the latter alone might suffice.

One provision is necessary, namely, that reports of those anthropologists be made available, preferably in published form, to all governments, missions, universities and training institutions concerned with, or interested in, the region. Not only will each administration and each mission benefit, but an examination of these reports, whether by mission or government anthropologists, with their bias towards application and the changing scene, may well reveal general principles of cohesion and development, which should be observed by administrations and missions.

Administrative Officers

Like missionaries, administrative officers, especially those responsible for native affairs in general, live in the midst of the natives in the administrative districts, visit native settlements as a matter of patrol-routine or to deal with emergencies, and are constantly in personal contact with native peoples. Unlike the missionaries, however, they do not remain many years in one district; moreover, their districts are much larger than any area for which one missionary endeavours to maintain personal contact, with the result that an officer seldom visits the greater part of his district more than once a year; further, as there are usually several languages in use in an administrative district, and as an officer expects to be moved to other districts in the course of his years of service, with few exceptions he does not learn a native language, but manages with a *lingua franca*, Motu, pidgin, simple English, Malay or such like, or relies on interpreters for giving administrative orders, for hearing complaints, and passing judgments and so on. Clearly then, unless a number of communicative and co-operating members of a native society become proficient in the *lingua franca*, the officer cannot hope to gain much understanding of the people or their culture; he will observe that certain types of events occur usually in certain apparent circumstances, but he will be very fortunate if he learns the real nature of the correlation or why events happen. Superstition will just be superstition to him; sorcery will be "obviously" ever-present terrifying imposture; and the social structure an intricate maze, in which he is satisfied to pick up an odd thread or two in order to settle some land or inheritance problem.

Consequently, books by administrative officers, and fortunately a goodly number have been written, while providing very interesting accounts of regions and peoples, of journeys and of administration, must be classed either as good explorers' journals, or as biographies, and only in a very few instances as providing any material of anthropo-sociological and practical value. One of the best is Beaver's *Unexplored New Guinea*; useful information can be mined from it, but it does not lead us to an understanding of any community, or of what was happening in or to it. Sir Hubert Murray's two books, *Papua or British*

New Guinea, and *Papua of To-day*, belong to this class, but they are of special value because of the discussion of principles of native administration, and of his recognition of the practical use of anthropology.

Some administrative officers, however, have made useful contributions to anthropology, but only because they had received some training in this discipline and kept up their interest in it. Articles by Mr. Leo Austen and Mr. Leigh Vial published in *Oceania* are examples; while from Netherlands officials in western New Guinea we expect something worth while, for they are thoroughly trained, even to Doctorate standard; unfortunately, however, they had not been at work very long in the region before the outbreak of the second World War.

Generally speaking we cannot expect administrative officers to undertake the detailed continuous sociological research in every part of their districts, though, if satisfactorily trained, they should produce occasional papers on some aspects of the culture and of the problems of change.

Settlers

The settler—be he planter, miner, storekeeper or anything else—is seldom equipped to study native society or culture, or to realize, let alone analyse, the effects of his own contacts with native communities; moreover, his interest and energy are given to making a living and profit, natives being but means, adjuncts, or nuisances; in addition, in some regions, it is contrary to the white settler's concept of his own class and dignity to show any interest in the way of life of his native employees, or even to converse with them.

For such reasons, these island regions have not produced amateur inquirers such as W. Curr, Brough Smyth, R. H. Mathews, A. W. Howitt, John Fraser, Mrs. L. Parker, W. E. Thonemann, Trooper Gason, F. J. Gillen and the very many settlers and pastoralists who sent in useful information to the first four on this list. The semi-nomadic Australian aborigine manages and is willing to be more communicative to his employer than is the case with the Papuan and Melanesian, and his employer is seldom averse to asking him about his rules and beliefs.

Consequently, the settler in the islands has contributed very little directly to our understanding of the peoples in whose way of life he has caused a revolution.

3

ANTHROPOLOGISTS

THE third group which has contributed to our knowledge of the island peoples consists of trained anthropologists. These can be divided into two classes, chiefly on the basis of period and interest.

The Collection of Data Approach

To the first belong workers like C. G. Seligman, *Melanesians of British New Guinea*; W. H. R. Rivers, *The History of Melanesian Society*; C. B. Humphreys, *The Southern New Hebrides*; Felix Speiser, *Südsee, Urwald, Kannibalen*; and D. Jenness and A. Ballantyne, *The Northern D'Entrecasteaux*.

Their work was of the survey and collection type. They methodically collected material on the social structure and various cultural aspects, mainly through interpreters, and as recorders of what was past or was about to pass. True, Rivers added an ethnological volume to his ethnographical one, and so his work was not simply descriptive. However, the time had not fully come when the field-workers sought to understand a society's culture as a whole, and its institutions, customs and beliefs as functionally related to that whole and to each other. W. E. Armstrong in his *Rossel Island* moves towards this ideal, at least as far as his study of the money system of the Island is concerned, but a two months' sojourn is not sufficient to gain understanding of how a society functions or of its culture as a process. A scientific approach, however, requires just this understanding, and it alone is of practical value.

The Functional Approach

The anthropology of the first two decades of this century, which in this region may be associated mainly with the names and influence of Haddon, Seligman and Rivers, had to be superseded by a more vital and dynamic approach. The first real impetus came from B. Malinowski. He had unrivalled opportunity during World War I to get to know thoroughly a people, its society and culture. As a result he

produced in 1922 a book, *Argonauts of the Western Pacific*, which made
the Trobriand Islanders live in the minds of the readers, and their
culture, made up of interrelated functioning parts, be seen as a whole.
His other books on the area filled out the picture. So well was it done
that a later anthropologist, an administrator or missionary, can from
these books so know the society and culture before going to the
Trobriands, that when he arrives, he sees nothing strange, but simply
the books in action: the matrilineal principle, the position of the
chiefs, the gardens and magic, yam houses and yam displays, incest
and suicide, the kula, and so on, and all inter-dependent. Thus, no
official or missionary has any excuse for not knowing the context in
which the individuals and groups move, nor the cultural factors which
make them what they are. The practical value of such work is therefore obvious.

One important aspect was omitted: a searching inquiry into the
history and effect of contact on the social structure, culture and population; for the present position of a people, as a result of contact, is
just as significant and essential for understanding and administration,
as is the reconstructed picture of what it was, or the picture of what it
is, apart from administrative, missionary and other contacts and inter-
ferences. Further, it is only through an analysis of the factors and
effects of contact, where there has been such, that an understanding of
the present condition of a people and its culture can be obtained.
Moreover, such analysis and understanding will provide practical
guidance for the future.

I have emphasized this matter, because the efforts of governments to
promote the welfare and development of native peoples by administrative, educational, economic and missionary activity may have
unfortunate results, unless they are made with as complete an understanding of the total conditions as scientific research can provide.
Anthropology was not in a position before the 1930's to perform this
task satisfactorily; but since then it has been gradually passing beyond
the stage of being solely a descriptive and classificatory science, to one
in which observation and description are part of the method by which
laws of integration and change can be determined. This involves study
of a society at different periods for the purpose of comparing its
conditions at such intervals, isolating the factors of change, examining
their effects, and seeking principles of change.

The excellent descriptions of the Malinowski type, though not necessarily of the "school", include works like R. F. Fortune, *Sorcerers of Dobu*; H. Powdermaker, *Life in Lesu*; R. Firth, *We, The Tikopia*; G. Bateson, *Naven*; M. Mead, *Growing up in New Guinea* and *Kinship in the Admiralties*; R. F. Fortune, *Manus Religion*; M. Mead, *Sex and Temperament in Three Primitive Societies*; B. Blackwood, *Both Sides of Buka Passage*; B. Deacon, *Malekula*; and J. Layard, *Stone Men of Malekula*. But whether or not these satisfy the canons of those who regard themselves as functionalists, they are still but descriptions of societies or institutions at a particular "moment" in time, and either free from, or abstracted from, factors of contact and change. It is therefore unsound to deduce from such descriptions alone, likely effects of contact. Administrative action; missionary zeal, with its prohibitions and indoctrination, and usurpation of native land or labour by settlers: these will, of course, have some effects on the culture and people. Moreover, on the basis of functional description, suggestions can be made as to where the effects are most likely to be evident, and what the reverberations might be.

This approach alone, however, will not indicate with any degree of reliability whether the effects will undermine the social structure or not, or so interfere with and split up the cultural pattern that, bereft of social sanctions and ideals and of the traditional motivations, the society will fall into a condition of moral and social chaos. Such things can happen, and have happened, but by no means in every case of contact. Therefore, what might be called anthropological or sociological histories of contact are urgently needed. For this reason, I emphasize (as I have done for several years) the return of anthropologists to the fields of their previous researches, to study the problem of social and cultural change in all its aspects. If they are not available, other trained workers should be sent to these fields. This is sound scientific procedure, for such temporarily spaced observations and analyses take the place, as far as this can be done, of controlled laboratory experiments in the physical sciences; and because the method is sound scientifically, it will reveal results on which reliance can be placed for practical purposes.

To sum up; the contributions of anthropologists in the south-west Pacific regions have been mainly of two types: first, the planned collection and recording of social and cultural phenomena; second, and later, the study of cultures as integrated, or at least interrelated, wholes. The first was not altogether unrelated to the second. Rivers realized the organic aspect of culture when he urged the substitution of new or other pursuits and objects for those prohibited by authorities; and Haddon drew attention to the administrator's need of understanding the significance and ramifications of customs in his emphasis on the practical value of anthropology.

The Time or Changing-Culture Approach

Likewise, there has been some approach to the third and present type of contribution which is required. The late F. E. Williams in *Orokaiva Society* and *Orokaiva Magic*, in *Papuans of the Trans-Fly* and *The Drama of Orokolo*, as well as in several of his smaller official reports and in articles in *Oceania* recognized the inadequacy of the synchronous functional method and sought for principles established more deeply in history and psychology. He, however, was a Government anthropologist (in Papua) of twenty years' experience, and because of his position, tried to develop an approach which would provide understanding of the causes of happenings and also sound and reliable advice and prediction. This, of course, is the task of all science. H. I. Hogbin's *Experiments in Civilization* is a definite and worthy attempt to analyse cultural change, though handicapped by a comparatively short sojourn in the particular field. The same anthropologist's post-war study of Busama, a village near Lae, the result of several periods of work there, is a study of the contact position in its many aspects, out of which some general principles governing contact should emerge. S. W. Reed's *The Making of Modern New Guinea* is a very suggestive socio-historical study.

More work, more intense and more localized research of this kind, is required; it should be carried out by persons trained in both anthropological and historical methods—a combination of disciplines which is not infrequent in the University of Sydney. Finally, the results of Professor Thurnwald's reports on his two periods of research in Buin, separated as they were by an interval of twenty-five years, need careful examination with further field-work in the same area by a worker with a knowledge of the language,—for another sixteen years have passed. To seize such a unique opportunity would be an excellent way of establishing this third method and period of anthropological method and objective. The field-work being undertaken in the Trobriands this year by Mr. Powell of London, mainly on an Emslie Horniman

Scholarship, and the projected return visit of Professor R. Firth to Tikopia, are part of the development of this period of research.[1]

This development has come at a very opportune time in the history of Native Policy and Administration, and indeed must be correlated with it. The development of both *pari passu* is interrelated. Anthropology is no longer antiquarian; nor is it merely descriptive in the very best sense of that term as used in "Natural History"; it is dynamic, diachronic, and concerned with culture and social structure as a process, which is subject to ascertainable laws. It is therefore capable of providing principles for application in spheres in which the future is involved in present action.

This being so, governments responsible for native peoples and the changes which are coming upon them, and missionary authorities also, should insist on anthropological research of this third type, and then see that its results are used. This means the appointment of a few government and mission anthropologists, as already suggested, to deal with the problems as they arise, and to advise the "practical" man in his work. In addition, governments are urged to ensure to independent research institutions and universities adequate funds to enable planned research to be carried out at selected sample areas in this vast region, such areas to be chosen according to some such scheme as will be outlined in Part III.

Plans of Research in the Past

Three main phases of professional field research have taken place in the New Guinea-Melanesia region. The first covered the period 1900 to about 1925, being ushered in by the Cambridge Expedition to Torres Straits in 1899. It included expeditions by Seligman and Landtman in Papua, Rivers, Hocart, Speiser and Thurnwald, mainly in the Solomons and the New Hebrides, J. Layard in the New Hebrides, and Malinowski, Jenness and Armstrong in Papua. Malinowski's work during the period of the first World War filled in what otherwise would have been an anthropological hiatus in the region.

The second phase received its impetus from the Pacific Science Congress of 1923, held in Melbourne and Sydney. The Netherlands, France, the United Kingdom and Australia were amongst the member countries of the Congress which were represented at this meeting. The

[1]Mr. Powell's work was completed, and Professor Firth returned to Tikopia in 1952.— A. P. E., November, 1952.

Congress recorded its opinion that the preservation, progress and welfare of the native population of Oceania could best be carried out by policies based on the investigation of native culture, and recommended that provision should be made for the teaching of anthropology in the universities of Australia, such teaching (a) to be given in co-ordination with geographical, historical, psychological, and anatomical departments; (b) to be a training for government officials, missionaries and others who would have personal contact with natives; and (c) to be a training for field-investigators, who might, or might not, be attached to some local government.

The Congress, further, urged governments responsible for the welfare of Oceanic peoples to "recognize that ethnology has a practical value in administration and is of definite economic importance," and to proceed without delay to take the necessary steps. It was also agreed that "for practical purposes, the investigation of various areas in Oceania should be undertaken as a whole by definite bodies." One of these areas was New Guinea and Melanesia; and it was suggested "that Australia should more particularly investigate Papua, the Mandated (now Trustee) Territory of New Guinea, and Melanesia, but the United Kingdom and France should assist in this work."[1]

The Australian National Research Council, being the Australian member of the Pacific Science Council, which is responsible for the Pacific Science Congresses, took the matter up with governments and institutions. As a result, a Department of Anthropology was established, at first solely on the basis of Government grants, in the University of Sydney in 1926. In addition the Rockefeller Foundation and the Carnegie Corporation made such generous grants to the Australian National Research Council that research in Papua, New Guinea and northern Melanesia (as well as in Aboriginal Australia) was begun almost at once, under the direction of the Research Council's Committee on Anthropology, of which the Professor of Anthropology was, and still is, Chairman. This work was continued almost until the outbreak of the second World War.

The Australian National Research Council sent fourteen expeditions into the region, and in addition, through the Chairman of its Anthropological Committee, co-operated with field-workers, in at least ten

---

[1]*Proceedings of the Pan-Pacific Science Congress, Australia*, 1923, Vol. 1, pp. 40-43. The other three areas in which anthropological research was recommended were Australia, Polynesia and Micronesia.

expeditions, who came from other research institutions abroad, in particular helping them in planning their field-work and in equipping themselves.[1]

Though, of course, twenty-four expeditions could only touch the fringe of the huge task to which the Pacific Science Congress called attention, yet work in well selected sample areas, in some cases done by workers with previous field-experience, made a very material and sound contribution to the anthropology of the region. For the most part it was not concerned with the problem of change.

The third phase commenced towards the end of the war, with the work of K. E. Read (Markham Valley) and H. I. Hogbin (Busama) and was being continued by the recent entry of three new field-workers into the region:—P. Lawrence at Sumau-Iwaiwa; Dr. C. S. Belshaw at Waga Waga (Milne Bay), Ware (Teste Island), and Port Moresby; and H. A. Powell on the Trobriands.

This phase, as I have urged, must become a definitely planned advance, both as to fields and problems. The recommendations made by the Pan-Pacific Congress of 1923 must be made again, but with a deeper meaning as to significance and with an added sense of urgency. One purpose of this survey of the region and of this plan of research is to do this.

---

[1]See, A. P. Elkin, "Research in Australia and the Pacific", 1927-37, *Oceania*, Vol. VIII, No. 3, pp. 313-315; also *idem*, "Anthropology and the Peoples of the South-west Pacific", *Oceania*, Vol. XIV, No. 1, pp. 1-3.

PART II

SURVEY OF ANTHROPOLOGICAL KNOWLEDGE OF
THE REGION, WITH SUGGESTIONS FOR RESEARCH
PROJECTS

4

INTRODUCTION

THIS survey is concerned mainly with our knowledge of the social structure and culture of the peoples in the region. I have already emphasized the importance of the former. It is the continuing framework in which the successive generations find their place, their security and their opportunity for social life. If it begins to break down, confusion follows. The breakdown can be caused by native "wars" and raids; by serious decrease of population, or by interference on the part of non-native administrative, missionary or employing authority. On the other hand, practical recognition of the structure can prevent its breakdown and even make changes possible without disaster.

By culture I mean the total complex of institutions, beliefs and customary ways of life, by which a people adjusts itself to its geographical and human problems. Culture is a process always handed down, and yet ever changing slightly, occasionally markedly in some aspect. The rate and range of change is increased by the contact of peoples, especially if one party to the contact is intent on making a change in the other's way of life. This is just the purpose of administrations and missions and to some extent of employers and traders. The problem is at what rate, and over how wide a range of the total culture (institutions, customs or habitual ways and beliefs) can these deliberate changes be effected, without causing maladjustment, uncertainty and confusion. The administering authority aims at native readjustment, but maladjustment and uncertainty can be so serious that depopulation (both deliberately or unconsciously induced), duplicity or nativistic movements can follow.

The anthropology to the point here is not concerned with the culture of peoples before contact for its own sake, though it is interesting to have records of what has gone or is going. This knowledge however, where available, does provide a basis for the study of culture-change in its various aspects. Our concern is not with anthropological archives, but with peoples in a process of change, the end or final direction of which we cannot be sure. Therefore, the survey is concerned with records of, and research projects into, native cultures irrespective of whether they were or are in a condition of pristine savagery. Indeed, we must beware lest a very good theoretical book based on sound field work leaves an impression of a condition of culture which actually has been greatly changed. Thus, Dr. R. F. Fortune's *Sorcerers of Dobu* needs to be read against the changing background provided by the Rev. W. E. Bromilow's *Twenty Years among Primitive Papuans*, 1929. On the other hand, Dr. Paul Wirz makes clear that the Marind-anim culture which he recorded (*Die Marind-anim*, 1922, 1925) was a thing of the past.

From this point of view, some missionaries with long experience in a district and in the use of its language, have already made valuable contributions, and could make many more, to our knowledge of the life of native peoples, as they experience it. In particular they could, as persons vitally interested, note and throw light on the latter's response and attitude to the changes to which they are subjected. That is, missionaries, and to a lesser extent administrative officers also, apart from any specialized ethnographical work which they might do, could help considerably in understanding the contact and change process, if they kept regular records of any changes in behaviour, attitudes and expressions of opinion observed by themselves. At the same time they should record (with dates and circumstances) all demands for changes in behaviour, values and forms of activity which they make on the natives. This does not mean that these observers will know what the natives are thinking or doing; nor does it mean that they will not be misled by apparent acquiescence. But they will preserve for later analysis by themselves or anthropologists a sequence of phenomena which will throw much light on native reactions and attitudes. This is of great practical value.

For the past, we can only draw upon the incidental references to such phenomena in missionary writings, such as J. Chalmers, *Work and Adventure in New Guinea*, 1885, which is quite helpful; and W. E. Bromilow's book, already mentioned.

The survey is not concerned with physical anthropology, though the distribution, origins and movements of racial types in the region is important scientifically. It is, however, seldom of any practical significance. Difference in culture and in language and geographical separation are more important, whether or not they are correlated with differences in appearance.

In spite of this, unless a physical anthropologist be available, in certain areas where there are obviously marked differences in types, as shown by average height, skin colour, head-form, countenance or hair form, the social anthropologist should, if only as a diversion, take a few stock measurements and observations, together with careful photographs, and link the different groups with his genealogical records. Wabag in the western Central Highlands is an example; there are many short people, some women being under four feet six inches, and many have a very light or reddish skin colour. The proportion of "pygmy" to "shortish" and to average, and the proportion of light-skinned to brown-skinned should be sought, and also their genealogical distribution.

The Survey

The survey commences on the west with Netherlands New Guinea, proceeds through Papua from west to east, then in the opposite direction for the "mainland" of the Trust Territory of New Guinea, thence across to Manus, back to New Britain, New Ireland and Kieta Administrative Districts; then southwards through the British Solomon Islands Protectorate, the New Hebrides and so to the Loyalty Islands and New Caledonia.

5

NETHERLANDS NEW GUINEA

ALTHOUGH one of the most studied peoples, the Marind-anim, is in Netherlands New Guinea, not much other systematic anthropological research has been carried out in it. This may be correlated with the presence of only a few non-native persons, settlers, officials and missionaries, until the 1930's. Salomon Mueller's *Reizen en Onderzoekingen in den Indischen Archipel*, 1e Deel: Bijdragen tot de Kennis van Nieuw-Guinea (pp. 1-128) gives a brief ethnographical description of the obvious objects, activities and customs of the natives seen on the south-west coast of Netherlands New Guinea in 1828. He was on the *Triton*, a Dutch corvette, on duty in the region.

In 1872, L. M. d'Albertis (*New Guinea: What I Did and What I Saw*, 1880, Vol. I, pp. 39-150), an ornithologist, spent some months amongst the natives on the north coast of the "Bird's Head". He worked mainly in the district of and inland from Andai, on the north-west coast of Geelvink Bay, where missionaries had been working since about 1863, and at Ramoi opposite the island of Salwattee (Salawati). He gives a brief description of the natives in both districts (pp. 210-219).

d'Albertis did not touch the south coast of Netherlands New Guinea. On the other hand, a German doctor (M. Krieger), a trained observer, gives (*Neu-Guinea*, pp. 364-439) in 1899 a general description of the natives and their life on various parts of the coast from Humboldt Bay in the north-east near what was then German New Guinea, to Geelvink Bay in the central north, McCluer Bay opposite, and the south-east from Princess Marianne Strait along the coast of the Tugeri, that is the Marind-anim. He linked his coastal survey with Kaiser Wilhelm Land on the north, and British New Guinea on the south.

A. Wichmann, "Entdeckungsgeschichte von Neuguinea", *Nova Guinea*, Vol. I, 1909, pp. 1-387; Vol. II, 1910, 1912, pp. 1-1026, describes the results of the expedition on the north coast, and also summarizes the results of previous expeditions.

On the north coast of Netherlands New Guinea, only one piece of intensive research has been completed (and published). Dr. J. Held, in *Papoea's van Waropen*, 1947, deals with all aspects of the society and culture of the Waropen on the east side of Geelvink Bay. He has also published a work on the language.

I. THE NORTH-EAST

Near the Trust Territory of New Guinea border, on the west of Lake Sentani, the Mission is studying the language of the Nimboran, who number about five thousand, and amongst whom a community development project is being carried out with the help of the South Pacific Commission. For this reason anthropological research should be done in the district, so that the background of social structure and culture should be understood, and the ramifications of the project recognized.

A basis was provided by P. Wirz ("Dies und jenes uber die Sentanier und die Geheimkulte im Norden von Neu-Guinea", *Tijdschrift voor de Taal-, Land -en Volkenkunde*, Batavia, Vol. 63, 1923, pp. 1-81. "Beitrag zur Ethnologie der Sentanier", *Nova Guinea*, Vol. 16, 1928, pp. 251-370). Earlier work by G. A. J. van der Sande, in the Wichmann Expedition, deals mostly with material culture (*Nova Guinea*, Vol. III, 1907, pp. 1-390).

Max Moskowski published in 1911 a brief report of an ethnographical expedition to the district near the mouth of the River Mamberamo and also up the river as far as the Van Rees Range. In the latter district he made contact with the Koassa, Kamboi-Ramboi, and Borumessu tribes.[1]

An exploratory expedition was made in 1920 up the Mamberamo River from the north coast. Dr. H. J. T. Bijlmer, a physician with the well-being of native peoples at heart, wrote a popular description of the people visited, mostly the Timorini (*Met de Centraal Nieuw-Guinee Expeditie*, 1920). As control and contact spreads into part of the interior by this route, an ethnographical survey and intensive research into sample groups are called for amongst the Middle and Upper Mamberamo tribes and its tributaries.

Paul Wirz also worked amongst the Timorini of the Swart Valley in 1921-22. ("Anthropologische und Ethnologische Ergebnisse der Central New Guinea Expedition 1921-22" *Nova Guinea*, Vol. XVI, 1924). The work of these two observers could almost be put in Region 5, the Interior Highlands.

[1] M. Moskowski: "Die Volkerstamme am Mamberamo in Holländisch-Neuguinea und auf den vorgelargerten Inseln"; *Zeitschrift für Ethnologie*, XLIII, 1911, pp. 315-46.

2. GEELVINK BAY

Moskowski, in the report just mentioned, when discussing the tribes at the mouth of the Mamberamo, said that they had come there from the Islands in the north of Geelvink Bay in the first decade of this century.

Some ethnographical data was obtained from Biak in an expedition in 1915-16 by Feuilletau de Bruijn (*Mededeelingden Encyclopaedisch Bureau*, 1920). Dr. J. V. de Bruijn (no relation to the preceding), an administrative officer, has studied the clan system of Biak villages for the purpose of determining land rights; he has also inquired into the Messiah Cult there. Some of his material has recently been published as an article, "De Mansren-cultus der Biakkers", in *Tijdschrift voor Ind. Taal-, Land- en Volkenkunde*, Dl. 83, Jaarg. 1949, pp. 313-330.

The Biak (including Numfoor) is the largest tribe in Netherlands New Guinea, certainly in the coastal regions. In the fifteenth century it spread to the northern coast of the "Bird's Head". There are also Biak clans on the north coast of Japen and on two smaller islands. The tribe numbers 31,000.

It is most important that the Biak should be studied intensively, concentrating on the islands of Biak and Numfoor. It is a very large and influential Papuan tribe. Moreover, the process of culture-change, because of the tribe's geographical position and its many contacts, has been rapid, especially in recent years. One symptom of this is its ever-present Cargo or Messiah Cult, which breaks out about every five years or so. This is stimulated by an originally indigenous Heil-bringer Cult, centred in Biak itself.

In addition, Biak and the Geelvink region in general were involved in the Japanese war, and the effect of various elements in this might well be a potent factor in the processes of change.

The population of the east coast of Geelvink Bay is about seven thousand. We have Professor Held's complete study of the Waropen. If there is to be any research in that region and in the rest of the coast of this Bay in the near future, it might well be confined to a survey of the present social, economic and cultural position, and, in the light of earlier, even though superficial, descriptions and of any reliable history which can be obtained, to determining the reaction to both time and contact, and also the general trends.

3. THE SOUTH-EAST

One other area has been well studied—the south-east coast near the Papuan border. There is a vast literature on the Marind particularly the Marind-anim. Dr. Paul Wirz, *Die Marind-anim von Holländisch-Süd-Neu-Guinea*, 1922, 1925 (2 volumes) will surely become a classic. It is a complete ethnographical description of a people and their country, their social, economic and religious life, their cults, head-hunting and sorcery, their "world-view" and their group-movements. But even at the date of publication the Marind-anim had ceased to exist as a community or people and their colourful culture was a thing of the past. Depopulation was serious.

The only reasons for further inquiry would be (1) to isolate, if possible, the causes of depopulation; (2) to give a functional picture of the present social structure and culture of the remnant; and (3) to indicate lines and methods for the recovery of the Marind-anim as a group, if such seems at all feasible.

In carrying out such research, amongst other literature to be consulted, Dr. J. van Baal's *Godsdienst en Samenleving in Nederlandsch-Zuid-Nieuw-Guinea*, 1934, would occupy a high place. On the basis of the literature, and also of his own field-work done since Wirz, Dr. van Baal examines the social organization, philosophy, religion, rites, cults and magic of the Marind-anim. Because of its strong psychological and interpretative character, his work aims at exposing the general trends of the culture. This type of theoretical study of a people can be of very real practical value. The author is an administrative officer and anthropologist at present in charge of native affairs and education in Netherlands New Guinea.

J. van Baal gives fifteen pages of Bibliography and P. Wirz seven pages for the area. The former also published an important article on culture-change and population in the same region.

For the Jee-, Mangat-, and Kanum-anim tribes between the Marind and Papua, Wirz obtained a little information, and it is probably too late to learn much more. The tribes to the north, however, on the Digul River and between it and Papua, are in good country. Some of them are nomadic. The Sacred Heart Mission is working in the region, using the Arau language.

As development is possible here, an anthropological knowledge of the people should be obtained.

West of the Marind-anim is Frederik Hendrik Island. For the Jab-anim and Makleeu-anim between the two, Wirz obtained some data, mainly about their totemic groups. For the island, the Mission has provided a little information on the village, hunting and gardening life of the natives, as well as on the geography of the Island. This, with vocabularies published by Fr. Drabbe, and the contacts made by the Mission furnish a basis for research. Probably, however, this should be carried out by a Mission anthropologist, unless the Administration decides to establish a post there. There seems to be little or no possibility of economic development. The northern part of this south-eastern region from Etna Bay, through the Digul along the foot of the mountains to about Tanah Merah, a vast swampy river area, is practically unknown, except for the Verslag der Militaire Exploratie 1907-1915.

4. THE CENTRAL-SOUTH

About two degrees west of the Marind-anim, the foundation has been laid for sociological research amongst the people of the Kamoro Plain, extending from the Karamuga River (137° 5′E.) to the Opa River (134° 15′E.). They are sometimes referred to as the Mimika, but not correctly. The language has been well studied by the Rev. P. Drabbe, a missionary in the area, and a long series of folk-tales has appeared in *Oceania*, 1947-9.

Earlier, Dr. A. F. R. Wollaston had given in *Pygmies and Papuans*, 1912, an account from the point of view of a very observant naturalist on an exploring expedition, of the near-nomadic Wakatimi Papuans on the lower Mimika, who had then experienced little external contact.

The work of this explorer and of Fr. Drabbe shows that this area is worth studying; the adaptation of the natives to their difficult and uninviting country is itself of scientific interest and reveals man's remarkable powers of adjustment. The change which has occurred since 1912 in their mode of life, mainly through missionary endeavour would also repay study. The area, however, is of no economic value to non-natives, but, of course, the well-being and progress of the natives are a matter of concern to the Government.

Dr. Wollaston, on the same expedition, pushing further up the Mimika to the foot-hills of the Nassau Range, visited and described a few Tapiro pygmies and one of their villages, Wamberimi. In

1934, Dr. Bijlmer visited this same pygmy region, but by going up the Kapare River slightly west of the Mimika.

Pygmies

Pygmies, wherever they are, are of scientific interest, both physically and culturally. We still need a thorough study and understanding of their way of life, and particularly of their beliefs, "world-views" and psychology. I urge that the opportunity be taken as soon as possible to study these Tapiro, and the other pygmy peoples further in the interior of New Guinea, such as the Pesechem of the Upper Lorentz, first seen by the H. A. Lorentz Expedition in 1910, and the Mt. Goliath pygmies, discovered by the military doctor, A. C. de Kock, in 1911 during a military exploring expedition.

References
A. F. R. Wollaston: *Pygmies and Papuans*, 1912.
H. A. Lorentz, *Zwarte Menschen Witte Bergen*, 1913, pp. 1-262.
C. G. Rawling: "Explorations in Dutch New Guinea" *Geographical Journal*, Vol. 38, 1911, pp. 233-52; same expedition as Wollaston's.
C. G. Rawling: *The Land of the New Guinea Pygmies*, 1913.
A. J. P. v.d. Broek: "Ueber Pygmaen in Niederländisch-Süd-Neu-Guinea" *Zeitschrift für Ethnologie*, Vol. XLV, 1913, pp. 23-44, summarizes Dr. Kock's material on the Mt. Goliath pygmies.
P. Drabbe: "Folk-tales from Netherlands New Guinea". *Oceania*, 1947-50, Vol. 18, Nos. 2, 3; Vol. 19, No. 1; Vol. 20, Nos. 1, 3.
S. Mueller: *Reizen en Onderzoekingen in den Indischen Archipel*, 1e Deel: Bijdragen tot de Kennis van Nieuw-Guinea, 1857, pp. 1-128.
P. Wirz: *Die Marind-anim Holländisch Süd-Neuguinea*, 1922, 1923.
C. C. F. M. Le Roux: *De Bergpapoea's van Nieuw-Guinea en hun Woongebied* Vol. I, 1948. Pp. 1-18, gives a summary of ethnographical exploration and discovery up to 1944.
A. C. Haddon: *Reports of the Cambridge Anthropological Expedition to Torres Straits*. Vol. I, 1935. General Ethnography; pp. 251-65, for a summary, with comments, of Wirz's *Die Marind-anim*.
J. van Baal: *Godsdienst en Samenleving in Nederlandsch-Zuid-Nieuw-Guinea*, 1934.
J. van Baal, "De Bevolking van Zuid Nieuw-Guinea an der Nederlandsch Bestuur: 36 jaren"; *Tijdschrift voor Indische Taal-Land-en Volkenkunde*, Vol. 79, Pt. 3, 1939.
H. Guertjens: "Frederik Hendrik Island". *Geographical Journal*, Vol. 81, 1933, pp. 435-8.
H. A. Lorentz: *Report of Military Expedition* 1907, 1915.
A. J. P. van der Broek: "Zur Anthropologie des Bergstammes Pesechem" *Nova Guinea*, Vol. VII, 1923.
J. W. V. Nouhuys: "Der Bergstamm der Pesegem im Innern von Niederländisch Neu-Guinea" *Nova Guinea*, Vol. VII, 1923.
H. J. T. Bijlmer: *Naar de Achterhoek der Aarde*, 1936.

5. THE INTERIOR HIGHLANDS

The interior highlands of Netherlands New Guinea are still in the main a closed book, from which the cover has only just been lifted.

The interior of the "Bird's Head", indeed, is only known by official reports, and remains to be studied anthropologically.

Wollaston and Bijlmer, as already mentioned, reported on the Tapiro pygmies on the upper waters of the Mimika and Kapare. Thirty or forty air miles to the north-west are the Wissel Lakes, which have been approached by following up the Jawe River and also by air, in the immediate pre-war years as well as during the war, by administrative officers (for example, Dr. J. V. de Bruijn—see also *Jungle Pimpernel* by Lloyd Rhys, 1947, pp. 1-239) and by missionaries. De Bruijn has valuable information about the Ekari and Migari tribes, but he has not been able to publish anything about them. C. C. F. M. Le Roux, however, who led the expedition to the area in 1939, has produced his report, *De Bergpapoea's van Nieuw-Guinea en hun Woongebied*, 1948-1950. The first volume (pp. 1-484) deals with the material culture, gardening and hunting and the related magic, mainly of the Dem tribe in the country between Lake Piniai and the Rouffaer River, with some reference also to the Ekari nearer the Lake. The second (pp. 485-1029)deals with the mental characteristics, social organization, religion, music, dance, birth to death, and language of the Dem, Moni, Ekari and Ndani. Some reference is made to the Simori. A good bibliography is given. Volume three contains 118 plates and 4 maps. Le Roux made use of the results of the earlier Stirling (American-Dutch) Expedition to the area in 1926. His base was on the Lakes from which he worked east to Debasiga and Humulai.

The population in this region is large, probably about 100,000. The Ekari alone number about 60,000, while the Kigani or Awembiak are 30,000 strong, and north of the River (Wabu) are the Wolari. The Ekari language is quite different from the Migani speech. On the other hand, the Mapia language spoken by the people up the Osiaso River, visited by Dr. Bijlmer, is the same as that used at the Wissel Lakes.

Both as a matter of scientific interest and in readiness for future development of the great district and population, anthropological work is definitely recommended. These people were almost completely isolated until the 1920's, and the contact has not yet been great. It would therefore be an excellent opportunity for studying a primitive culture which has undergone little modification.

De Bruijn's war-time work and the two missionary enterprises established at the Lakes provide a starting point both for a study of the society as it is, and of the effects of the degree of contact experienced through these agencies and indirectly, through other tribes, with the coast. This project could link up with and deepen the work done by Le Roux amongst the Dem, for his interests, as a museum director, were not primarily sociological.

6. THE BALIEM

Further east is another great region, also part of the interior highlands, the Baliem River whose full course has not yet been explored. In one valley alone a population of 60,000 was estimated. The tribe is the Ndani, referred to as the Big Ndani. The only report on them and the country is that of the Archbold Expedition (1938) which alighted by Catalina flying boat on the River itself. As an officer is to be posted in the district, provision should be made at the same time for anthropological research, both to assist in the forming and implementing of policies, and also to study carefully in all stages the process of cultural change which will follow.

7. THE ORANJE AND STERREN RANGES

Similarly, by reason of complete isolation until now, and also because contact influences, administration, missions and economic development are always imminent, the great triangular region north of these ranges should be studied as soon as penetration has been made. Nothing is known of the region or its people. It may include nomads and pygmies. It is quite possible that the Telafomin culture of the Upper Sepik extends across the border into this Netherlands highland region.

Further, on the southern slopes of the Oranje, near Mt. Goliath, is a pygmy people, about whom little is known.

SUMMARY FOR NETHERLANDS NEW GUINEA

To sum up: In Netherlands New Guinea there is a great opportunity for research in social and cultural anthropology, and a great practical need to get it done. The essential projects, roughly in order of priority, may be listed as follows:

1. The Biak-Geelvink Bay culture-contact and stress, and Cargo Cult area.

2. The Nimboran tribe because of the community development project.

3. The Wissel Lakes District where contact processes are in operation.

4. The Baliem, which is to be controlled.

5. The middle and upper Mamberamo.

6. The Wakatimi Nomads and the Tapiro pygmies north of them.

7. The Pesechem and Mt. Goliath pygmies.

8. The upper Digul country.

9. The region north of the Oranje and Sterren Ranges, as soon as penetrated.

10. The interior of the "Bird's Head".

11. A survey of the south-east to study the present social and cultural adjustment, and the population trend.

TERRITORY OF PAPUA

I. THE WESTERN DIVISION[1]

The Trans-Fly

PASSING into Western Papua, we have the poor Trans-Fly country with its relatively low and decreasing population of under 6,000. The main anthropological research there has been well done by the late Dr. F. E. Williams, for about twenty years Papua's Government Anthropologist. In his *Papuans of the Trans-Fly*, 1936, based on field work visits in 1926, 1928, 1930 and in 1932, and in his article "Rain-making on the River Morehead", 1929, he gives a reliable account and analysis of the organization, manner of life, head-hunting, magic and religion of the tribes on the east of the Marind or Tugeri, as they are locally known. These tribes are the Semariji, Gambadi, Wiram, Keraki, Mikud and the Kuramangu. Dr. Williams concentrated chiefly on the Keraki. Earlier information of a descriptive nature was given by L. M. d'Albertis (*New Guinea: What I Did and What I Saw*, 1880, Vol. II) about the natives of Moatta (Mawata) and Kiwai in 1875-77; by the Rev. J. Chalmers, about his first meeting with the Bugi (Bugilai or Buji) at the mouth of the Mai Kussa, at the beginning of the century; and by Mr. W. N. Beaver, an administrative officer, who in *Unexplored New Guinea*, 1920, relates his observations on, and experiences with, the coastal tribes from the border eastward to the Aird and Kikori.

The population, 1950, for the Trans-Fly (and Oriomo) is 3,725 males and 2,147 females—a not very satisfactory picture. Moreover, there is emigration to Netherlands New Guinea.

The Upper Fly

Actually in the years before the first World War the Western and Delta Divisions of Papua were officially considered to comprise most of the unknown parts of the Territory of Papua, and expeditions revealed the scattered nature of the population. An expedition in

[1]The administrative divisions referred to in this book are those of 1950.

1911-12 revealed little or no population between the Kikori and the Strickland, certainly not sufficient to justify the establishment of a government station in the region. Exploration was continued by administrative officers during the years of the first World War and in the 1920's and 1930's, with the result that some descriptive information about the peoples met became available in the official reports of their journeys, in articles and books. For example, Mr. Leo Austen (administrative officer) wrote on the Ok-Tedi River District in the far north-western corner of the Territory in 1923, describing its natives, their material culture and gardening; and amongst other writings are J. Hides' *Papuan Wonderland*, 1936; and Ivan Champion's *Across New Guinea From the Fly to the Sepik*, 1932.

No intensive research has yet been carried out in the inland of the Western Division, but the houseless, nomadic bow-and-arrow hunters and sago-eaters of the Rentoul, referred to by Hides, being aberrant for Papuans, should be studied at the first opportunity, both out of scientific interest, and also for the special problems peoples of such type of culture present to an administration intent on their development. Moreover, the search for oil, with its actual and possible contacts, provides both the opportunity and necessity for such anthropological research.

Need has also arisen for an anthropological survey and census, and for the selection of one, if not two, sample areas for intensive research in the Lake Murray and Upper Fly River region. An administrative post was established in 1947 at Maua on Lake Murray, amongst the head-hunters, and the Unevangelized Field Mission has moved up the Fly River beyond Madiri and established an outpost at Daviumbo at the junction of the Fly and Tedi, and one at Lake Murray. The social structure and culture as well as the language should be studied, and guidance given to the Mission in the early days of its work there, as a basis for positive administration and education in the Lake Murray district. In the far north-west corner, research should be carried out amongst the peoples of the Ok-Tedi or Alice River on the Netherlands New Guinea border and this work linked up with research both on the Netherlands side, and also in what may be loosely called the Telafomin area of the Trust Territory, although the latter will certainly require another research-worker, if only because of the formidable geographical barriers between it and the Papuan side.

Possibly some co-operative research could be carried out by Dutch

and Australian anthropologists in north-west Papua and the neighbouring districts of Netherlands New Guinea. It is interesting to notice
that whereas in the south migration is moving west across the political
boundary, in the north the movement is in the opposite direction.

The population on the Papuan side is not great. For the middle Fly
it is 1,385, while 4,000 is the present estimate for Kiunga, the Lake
Murray district, and 1,000 for Bosama.

References
    F. E. Williams: *Papuans of the Trans-Fly*, 1936, pp. i-xxxvi, 1-452. Introduction by
A. C. Haddon.
    F. E. Williams: "Rainmaking on the River Morehead". *J.R.A.I.*, LIX, 1929, pp.
379-98.
    Rev. J. Chalmers: "Notes on the Bugilai, British New Guinea". *J.A.I.*, Vol. XXXIII,
1903, pp. 108-10.
    Leo Austen: "The Tedi (Alice) River Country and the People Inhabiting It". In
Papua Annual Report, 1921-22, pp. 134-40.
    Leo Austen: "The Tedi River District of Papua". *Geographical Journal*, Vol. 62, 1923,
pp. 335-49.
    Leo Austen: "Report of a Patrol from Wukpit Camp (Tedi River) to Star Mountains
(from 6° S. to C.5° 15″ S.)". In *Papua Annual Report*, 1922-23. App. 3, pp. 27-37.

To return to the coast and the mouth of the Fly River: the Kiwai,
including their western division, the Mawata (from the Pahoturi River
to the Oriomo River), have attracted attention for a long time, partly
because the country and the mouth of their great river were not far
from the Torres Straits Islands, and the same mission, the London
Missionary Society, was interested in those islands and in the whole
of southern Papua. Its representatives did much exploratory work
along the coast from the 1880's onward. L. M. d'Albertis' ornitholo-
gical expeditions to the Fly River in 1875-77 grew out of interest
roused by missionary exploration. The Cambridge Expedition to
Torres Straits in 1899, under the inspiration of A. C. Haddon, increased interest in the cultures of the coast of the Western Division,
for Haddon sought to determine the sources and routes of diffusion
of culture traits.

Out of this background came the Rev. J. Chalmers' brief "Notes on
the Natives of Kiwai Island" in 1903, and he was a good observer;
Haddon's article on children's games on Kiwai; and then G.
Landtman's *The Kiwai Papuans of British New Guinea*, based on field-
work in 1910-1912, under the guidance of Westermarck and Haddon.
He also contributed articles on cats-cradles, war-magic, and folk-tales
during 1914-17. The Rev. E. Baxter Riley's *Among Papuan Headhunters*, 1925, and his record of origin myths as told and written by

Kiwai natives, 1931, serve with the rest to provide a record of this interesting people. P. Wirz (1934) in a survey of the culture of the Papuan Gulf region, regards the Kiwai as a focal point in a culture stream which spread east over the whole of this Gulf region.

Population (1950): Kiwai   2,239 (m); 2,159 (f): 4,398.

Oriomo, 1,253 (m);   964 (f): 2,217.

References

Rev. J. Chalmers: "Notes on the Natives of the Kiwai Islands, Fly River, British New Guinea". *J.A.I.*, Vol. XXXIII, 1903, pp. 117-24.

A. C. Haddon: "Notes on Children's Games in British New Guinea". *J.A.I.*, Vol. XXXVIII, 1908, pp. 289-97.

G. Landtman: "Cat's Cradles of the Kiwai Papuans, British New Guinea". *Anthropos*, Vol. IX, 1914, pp. 221-32.

G. Landtman: "The Magic of the Kiwai Papuans in Warfare". *J.R.A.I.*, Vol. XLVI, 1916, pp. 322-33.

G. Landtman: *The Kiwai Papuans of British New Guinea.* Introduction by A. C. Haddon. 1927, pp. i-xxxix, 1-485.

G. Landtman: "The Origins of Sacrifice as Illustrated by a Primitive People". In *Essays Presented to C. G. Seligman*, 1934, pp. 103-12.

E. B. Riley: *Among Papuan Headhunters*, 1925, pp. 1-316.

E. B. Riley: Some Myths of Origin from the Fly River, New Guinea: Told and written by natives of Kiwai, translated by E. Baxter Riley. *Mitteilungen der Anthropologischen Gesellschaft in Wien*, Vol. LXI, 1931, pp. 323-30. Introduction and notes by Sidney H. Ray.

P. Wirz: *Beiträge zur Ethnographie des Papua-Golfes, Britisch-Neuguinea.* Abhandlungen und Berichte der Museen für Tierkunde und Völkerkunde zu Dresden, Vol. XIX, 1934, pp. 1-103.

The Bamu

East of the Fly River is the Bamu, with its tributary, the Aramia. On both sides of the lower Aramia and extending south to the Fly is the Gogodara tribe (also referred to as Kabiri and Girara). Mr. A. P. Lyons has given (1926) a brief description, based on official visits from about 1913 onwards, of the people, their organization, various customs, and in particular their canoe-making and the Gi ceremony. Haddon included further information from Mr. Lyons on this tribe in an article (1916) and Mr. Beaver gives a short general account in *Unexplored New Guinea.*

Between the estuaries of the Fly and Bamu Rivers is Wabuda Island. A. P. Lyons in the *Annual Report for Papua*, 1913-14 (p. 181) gives a brief description of the customs of the Dekoro-Koromo people on this island. The same official wrote (1921) a short paper on the beliefs of the Bina tribe of the Bamu estuary.

No intense sociological or even complete descriptive study has been made of these people, nor does it seem necessary at present, in spite of the fact that an ex-Royal Papuan constable recently inspired a Cargo Cult among the Gogodara.

Population (1950): Gogodara, 2,437 (m); 2,737 (f): 5,174.

Bamu, estimate: 3,000.

Gama, estimate: 1,000.

References

A. P. Lyons: "Notes on the Gogodara Tribe of Western Papua". *J.R.A.I.*, LVI, 1926, pp. 329-60.

A. P. Lyons: *Annual Report for Papua*, 1913-14, pp. 99, 100, 181.

A. C. Haddon: "The Kaviri or Giraia District, Fly River, Papua". *J.R.A.I.*, XLVI, 1916, pp. 334-52.

W. N. Beaver: *Unexplored New Guinea*, 1920, pp. 188-209.

A. P. Lyons: "Animistic and other Spiritualistic Beliefs of the Bina Tribe, Western Papua". *J.R.A.I.*, LI, 1921, pp. 428-37.

P. Wirz: *Beiträge zur Ethnographie des Papua-Golfes, Britisch-Neuguinea*, 1934, pp. 1-103.

The Turama

East of the Bamu we find the Turamarubi—the Turama people consisting of six tribes, Doriomo, Umaidai (including the Auwarubi), Wariadai (on the west bank), Morigi and Haragu on Morigi Island, and Nabio on the eastern bank near Jukes Point. Mr. Leo Austen, formerly Administrative Officer, who spent three years in the Delta Division and several years in the Western Division, has commenced a series of articles in *Mankind* (Sydney) which will give a very good basis, as he says, for more intense work. He has so far described the characteristics and temperament of the people, some of the changes wrought by administration, their clans, food, trade and the Long House; and, in *Oceania*, 1936, their Head Dances. He has also discussed the locations, dialects, affinities and movements of the neighbouring tribes. These include the Baru (a semi-nomadic tribe) of the Turama estuary and south to the Gama; the Tamai inland between the Gama and the Bamu; the Kasere, a group of bush tribes on the east of the Turama; the Paiya (speaking Kerewa) on the west of the Omati estuary; east of the Omati, the Kerewa in the Kikori delta, speaking a dialect of Kiwai; and further east still, the Gopi and Urama ("both of whom must have come originally from the Fly River"—L. Austen).

Mr. Austen has also recorded (1932) a hero-legend which is widespread from Boiga Island east to the Purari; and Dr. P. Wirz discusses the extension of a certain type of cult (Kaiamuni etc.) from the Fly River to the Purari.

It is clear that Mr. Austen's researches, carried out in the 1920's,

could form the basis for a study (1) of culture-change and the movement of peoples, (2) of the relationship of tribes, clans and languages
from the Bamu to the Kikori, (3) of the differences in temperaments,
attitudes and values amongst groups in one region, and (4) of the social
structure and culture of a selected tribe. Included in (1) would be an
analysis of the effects of missionary and administrative contact.

Population: The Kerewa language, also known as the Goaribari, is
said by the London Missionary Society Mission to be understood by
12,000 people. An intense sociological study through the Kerewa
language, therefore, would be warranted and of practical value.
Actually in the controlled area of the Delta Division the 1950 census
gives 13,804 counted and another 900 estimated. A further estimate of
8,000 is made for the semi-controlled and uncontrolled parts of the
Division.

References

E. R. Oldham: "Gama-Turama District". *Papua Report*, 1922-3, p. 17.
Leo Austen: "Head Dances of the Turama River". *Oceania*, Vol. VI, No. 3, 1936,
pp. 342-50.
Leo Austen: "Notes on the Food Supply of the Turamarubi of Western Papua".
Mankind, Vol. 3, No. 8, Sydney 1946, pp. 227-30.
Leo Austen: "Notes on the Turamarubi of Western Papua". *Mankind*, Vol. 3, No. 12,
1947, pp. 366-74; Vol. 4, No. 1, 1948, pp. 14-23.
Leo Austen: "Legends of Hido". *Oceania*, Vol. II, No. 4, 1932, pp. 468-76.
P. Wirz: "The Kaiamuni-Ebiha-Gi-Cult in the Delta Region and Western Division
of Papua". *J.R.A.I.*, LXVII, 1937, pp. 407-13.
P. Wirz: *Beiträge zur Ethnographie des Papua-Golfes, Britisch-Neuguinea*, 1934, pp. 1-103.

2. THE DELTA DIVISION

Inland

Very little information is available about the peoples in the inland of
this Division. Consideration should be given to a survey and study of
the Bush Tribes "behind" Kikori on the Utuli River and Mali Creek.
The two main tribes are the Dumu (also called Kairi, which means
Bushmen) and the Poromi on their east. They differ from the Kerewa
as regards dwellings and the form of the men's house, but nothing is
known of their social structure and culture.

North of the Bevan Rapids on the Kikori is the Pavaia-speaking
people, possibly several thousand in number, but anthropologically
unknown. They are making some contact with civilization by coming
in small numbers to work at the sawmill at Port Romilly, and by
experiencing gaol at Bomana near Port Moresby for such offences as

tribal warfare. They might well be included in a general anthro-pological survey and census, which is required in all those regions, at least where there is no call for an intensive piece of research. More-over, the shortage of trained workers means that only a limited number of districts and peoples can be selected for such intensive research.

Passing east to the Mt. Murray District, we have a report of a patrol in 1921 by L. A. Flint (Assistant Resident Magistrate) through the Samberigi Valley, in which he describes his visit to 44 villages, divided amongst 8 tribes, the Bara, Samberigi, Siri, Tugi, Toraba, Ro, Keai and the Rorugi (or Woioba). He enumerated 47 Dubus, 629 houses, and a population of 3,378. The Samberigi, which is divided into three groups, the Okami, Foraga and Kerabi, numbered 1,630. Dr. Capell has recently obtained a little information about a Samberigi dialect spoken in Sau village of the Foraga group. In the Report for 1922-23, the Resident Magistrate (Mr. E. R. Oldham) gives some further notes on the people of this valley, but there our knowledge seems to stop. The district is seldom visited.

Kutubu District

On the Central Highlands on the Papuan side is the Lake Kutubu District, which was formerly in the Delta Administrative Division. Culturally too, the peoples around the Lake belong to the general cultural "circle" of the Delta rather than to the highland tribes to the north. On the other hand, the Grasslanders, as F. E. Williams called the people on the Augu, to the north-east of the Lake, have close cultural affinities with the highland tribes.

F. E. Williams has given a good introductory description of the Kutubu, who only numbered about 400. The Mubi, Fimaga and Ifigi tribes on the Mubi are allied in language and culture, the first alone being more populous and thriving than the Kutubu. He suggested that the Foi and Kafa further to the south-east probably belong to the same cultural group. At any rate coastal shells and an important cult have come to the Kutubu through these south-eastern groups. Further, the Fasu and Kaibu to the south-west of the Lake are in close touch with the Kutubu and have influenced their culture.

The Kutubu District thus presents a useful opportunity for anthro-pological research. There are a number of "related" tribes whose cultural connexions are with the coast of the Papuan Delta Division, and the overall population is sufficiently numerous to warrant investigation. Further, the contact so far has not been disruptive, but has been such as to smooth the way for the anthropologist. An earlier police camp is being replaced by an assistant district officer's station. Dr. Williams has worked there, and a mission (Unevangelized Field Mission) has just been established at the Lake. Further, there is a suggestion that the station might be shifted to a more populated centre north of the Lake. If so, this would make it more feasible for the investigator to move north-west to the Tari River and Tarifuroro on the north, and north-east to the Waga River, and so break into the Highland culture. A quite recent patrol to the districts north-east of Lake Kutubu, beyond the Augu, has shown an increasing readiness to accept the white man's presence.

References

    L. A. Flint: "Report on the Patrol through the Samberigi Valley, Mt. Murray District, Delta Division". *Papua Report* 1921-22, pp. 141-52.
    E. R. Oldham: "The Samberigi Valley". *Papua Report*, 1922-23, p. 8.
    F. E. Williams: "Group Sentiment and Primitive Justice". *American Anthropologist*, Vol. 43, No. 4, 1941, pp. 523-39.
    F. E. Williams: "Natives of Lake Kutubu, Papua". *Oceania*, Vol. XI, Nos. 2, 3, 4, 1940-41, pp. 121-58, 259-95, 374-402. Vol. XII, Nos. 1, 2, 1941, pp. 49-75, 134-55. (Reprinted as Oceania Monograph, No. 6).
    F. E. Williams: "The Grasslanders". *Papua Report*, 1938-39, pp. 39-67.

South-east of the Delta Division

Returning to the coast, and moving east from the Kikori, we pass to the Purari Delta District, which, thanks to the Rev. J. H. Holmes and Dr. F. E. Williams, is comparatively well known. Mr. Holmes was twenty years in the region before writing *In Primitive New Guinea*, 1924. Dr. Williams' field study was done in 1922. Sir Hubert Murray visited the District often and refers to it in his *Papua or British New Guinea*, 1912; information is also given in J. Chalmers' *Pioneering in (British) New Guinea*, 1887, and T. F. Bevan, *Toil, Travel and Discovery in British New Guinea*, 1890, (especially pp. 188-207).

According to Williams, the census of 1917 gave the population of the coastal villages of the Purari Delta group, known as the Namau, as 8,686. However, the number of Delta people now speaking the Namau language, or dialects of it—dialects which are becoming merged—is reckoned by Dr. Capell to be about 20,000. Some of the villages contain from 1,500 to 2,000 persons.

Williams grouped the Namau into four tribes: the Koriki (also called Ukiravi)—the whole group is tending to-day to be known as the Korimi; the Iari; the Kaimari (which is allied with the Maipua and Vaimuru villages); and the Baroi. The Namau had very little knowledge of inland tribes, but their interests and ideas have been changed, especially right on the coast, by men who have returned from work outside their own district—and there are many such men. Dr. Capell has reported that these have caused considerable changes in diet, manner of living and disposition of houses—changes which were not due to missionary influence; indeed this last has been very slight, partly because of insufficiency of mission staff, and partly, I would suggest, because of the separatist and difficult nature of the Delta terrain of mud. Observation suggests that the natives want to better their conditions, and with a uniformity of language, a community centre in the Ravi ("club"-house) and interest in outside affairs, the opportunity for advance is present, as Dr. Capell urged in his *Report on Linguistic Investigation of Papua*[1], 1947. The reported (1950) abolition of Long Houses and carvings is probably a backward step—perhaps only temporary.

It is therefore encouraging to know that a "community development project" has been approved by the Director of Education, Papua and New Guinea, for a selected village, Iari, in the Romilly-Purari Delta District, on the basis of a practically spontaneous urge. The essential anthropological and linguistic research has been done. Once the project is under way[2], a sociologist, working in Namau language, could make a useful contribution by studying the effects of the project on social structure, important aspects of the culture, and on attitudes. Any such project is an experiment; all experiments should be observed in detail throughout the process, so that causes and effects can be distinguished and correlated. This is a scientific duty; it is also just as important from the point of view of native progress.

References

J. H. Holmes (Rev.): "A Preliminary Study of the Namau Language, Purari Delta, Papua". *J.R.A.I.*, Vol. XLIII, 1913, pp. 124-42.

J. H. Holmes: *In Primitive New Guinea*, 1924, pp. 1-305. Introduction by A. C. Haddon.

[1]This began as a research project from the University of Sydney, Department of Anthropology, but at the request of Mr. W. C. Groves, became a project undertaken to assist the Department of Education, Papua-New Guinea.

[2]This project is now (November 1952) being carried out. It is a project with which the South Pacific Commission is associated.—A. P. E.

J. H. Holmes: *Wayback in Papua*, 1926, pp. 1-320.

F. E. Williams: "The Natives of the Purari Delta". *Anthropological Report*, No. 5, 1924, pp. 1-270.

F. E. Williams: "Pairama Ceremony in the Purari Delta". *J.R.A.I.* Vol. LIII, 1923, pp. 361-87.

F. E. Williams: "The Collection of Curios and the Preservation of Native Culture". *Anthropological Report*, No. 3, 1923, pp. 1-23.

A. Capell: *Report on Linguistic Investigation of Papua*. 1947. Typescript only.

3. THE GULF DIVISION

The Gulf Division of Papua will always be notable in the world of anthropology for two reasons: the outbreak of the "Vailala Madness" in 1919, and the appearance of F. E. Williams' delightful book, *The Drama of Orokolo*, in 1940. There will be a third reason: the remarkable length of the great Toaribi legends, of which I hope to publish at least one example in *Oceania* in the near future.

Very little is known about the people of the rugged interior, who are simply called Kukukuku, a word meaning "tobacco-tobacco". Soldiers working on the road from the Lakekamu River met numbers of them and remarked on their short stature. Some have worked recently for the Australian Petroleum Company on the Upper Vailala. Some references are made to them in Annual Reports, their mobility, that is, nomadic propensity, being especially noted. Apparently they do not possess a permanent village system. However, the ruggedness of the country, the Kukukuku's way of life, their shyness of us, and our almost complete ignorance of them, not only would make research difficult at present; it also renders it unnecessary from a practical point of view. However, they are slowly making contact; therefore, we must be ready to make a survey of their locations, dialects, and general manner of life, together with a census. This will have an important bearing on their future, and determine whether sociological research is needed. The Annual Report for 1948-49 (p. 11) stated that there were no patrols inland amongst the nomadic Kukukuku, "but there is now a total of seven village constables among these people, a number of whom are becoming static and are building permanent villages near the coast and in the Lohiki area on the Vailala River."

In addition to the Kukukuku in the inland, about 2,000 people, called the Yaraga and the Kaverope have been contacted recently between Kerema and the Tauri River.

The Elema

On the coast of this Division Dr. Capell distinguishes three main groups from a linguistic point of view: (1) Orokoro, spoken or understood by 12,000 or more, (while east of the lower Vailala and at the back of Kerema, a divergent dialect of Orokoro (Orokolo) is spoken by what seems to be a great number); (2) Kerema, by about 3,000; and (3) Toaripi, by possibly 10,000 people, from just east of Kerema to the border of the Central Division. The recent census gives west Kerema (Erava to Parakou) as 12,637, and east Kerema (Huma to Vailala East) as 9,222.

F. E. Williams regards the whole coast as a group of about ten tribes called the Elema, with definite differences, but linked by several social and cult elements. The *Papua Annual Report*, 1948-49, p. 11, speaks of these "fairly well advanced coastal tribes among whom there is great similarity in type and customs, being divided into six main groups, viz., Orokolo, Vailala, Keuru, Mei, Motumotu and Toaripi." Dr. Williams' writings, *The Drama of Orokolo*, with its introduction on the social and tribal structure, *Bullroarers, Trading Voyages*, and *Seclusion and Age-grouping in the Gulf of Papua*, afford a sound background for understanding the Elema. To these can be added the earlier short accounts by the Rev. J. Holmes in 1902 on their religious ideas and initiation ceremonies, ancestry and country, and by W. R. Humphries, Resident Magistrate, in 1926 (on the Ehalo ceremony) in Koraita village.

Much iconoclasm has been associated with mission work in the Orokolo end of the coast, the men's house (*eravo*) and the Heveho ceremony being almost relegated to the past, though amongst the Toaripi in the east the Semese (Heveho) ritual has been performed in recent years. The present missionary attitude, however, favours the retention of what was valuable in the past. In addition, we must bear in mind the usual effort made by native peoples of about the third generation of contact "to return to", or "to recapture" as much of their own past as possible, so that they might feel themselves to be a "people", as well as to be psychologically secure. It is therefore essential that the general education policy and also missionary policy should take full cognizance of the essentials of the social structure and of the people's cultural values. The degree to which elements of the "past" are functioning varies along the Elema coast, and sociological research should aim at ascertaining and analysing functionally what these are, and their present strength. Lacunae, if any, should be noted. In other words, here as in many other sub-regions, social and cultural stock-taking is needed, especially in the light of a forward policy of native development.

Whether or not Cargo Cults are likely to arise in this sub-region is not an easy matter to determine, but it is tied up here as elsewhere with contact relations—with the degree in which fulfilment coincides with anticipated material acquisitions resulting from the contact, and with the loss of integrating elements of the culture. The Vailala Madness arose in the western part of this Division and spread to Ipisi, a Kerema village; but the village of Orokolo, retaining at the time (1919) its great cults, was not affected, although the phenomenon was referred to in an early report as the "Vailala or Orokolo Kava-Kava" (madness). It did not affect the Toaripi. The whole of the Elema coast has experienced much contact with whites of many types, and a knowledge of their opinion of us might be very enlightening. André Dupeyrat (p. 501) writing in 1935, pointed out that what mission-teaching these people had received had been a varnish which made their pagan culture more redoubtable. Moreover, many of the natives had learnt to be knavish towards whites, flattering or deceiving them, nor was their opinion of the "whites" raised by their contacts with those who sought for gold (Lakekamu) and oil (Vailala) in the Division. Attitudes play a potent part in the contact position, and have special bearing on education.

References

J. Holmes (Rev.): "Initiation Ceremonies of Natives of the Papuan Gulf". J.A.I., Vol. 32, 1902, pp. 418-25.

J. Holmes: "Notes on the Religious Ideas of the Elema Tribe of the Papuan Gulf". J.A.I., Vol. 32, 1902, pp. 426-31.

J. Holmes: "Notes on the Elema Tribe of the Papuan Gulf". J.A.I. Vol. 33, 1903, pp. 125-34.

J. Holmes: "Introductory Notes on the Toys and Games of Elema, Papuan Gulf". J.A.I., Vol. 38, 1908, pp. 280-8.

W. R. Humphries: "Ehalo Ceremony". Papua Report, 1925-6, pp. 16-18.

F. E. Williams: "Bull-Roarers in the Papuan Gulf". Anthropology Report No. 17, 1936, pp. 1-55,.

F. E. Williams: "Seclusion and age grouping in the Gulf of Papua". Oceania, Vol. IX, No. 4, 1939, pp. 359-82.

F. E. Williams: Drama of Orokolo, 1940, pp. 1-446.

F. E. Williams: "Trading Voyages from the Gulf of Papua". Oceania, Vol. III, No. 2, 1932, pp. 139-66.

"The Vailala Movement". *Papua Report*, 1919-20, pp. 29-30.

G. H. Murray: "The Vailala Madness". *Papua Report*, 1919-20, pp. 116-18.

F. E. Williams: "The Vailala Madness and the Destruction of Native Ceremonies in the Gulf Division". *Anthropological Report*, No. 4, 1923, pp. 1-72.

F. E. Williams: "The Vailala Madness in Retrospect". *In Essays Presented to C. G. Seligman*, 1934, pp. 369-79.

André Dupeyrat: *Papouasie: Histoire de la Mission* (1885-1935), 1935, pp. 1-542.

4. THE CENTRAL DIVISION

Although this part of Papua has been long settled, at least on the coast and in some inland districts, and has been the scene of much missionary and administrative activity during the past seventy years, not much intensive anthropological research has been done in it. The probable explanation was that where research was possible the old culture had been broken down, and by the time C. G. Seligman had gathered up the fragments in 1910, among the Roro and Mekeo, it was thought that there was nothing left to do; further, the interior was very difficult and forbidding country, and the people too scattered. So descriptions by missionaries and patrol officers, usually brief, and the heroic achievement of R. W. Williamson amongst the Mafulu in 1910 under Haddon's inspiration, sufficed. The importance of a sociological study of a people as it is in the process of contact and change had not been fully realized. Anthropology was confined too much to a recapture or a study of culture before contact.

In the western part of this Division, we have Seligman's study of the social structure and some aspects of the culture of the Roro and their Mekeo neighbours. This is the basic and systematic work. There is, however, some useful earlier writing: L. M. d'Albertis, the naturalist, records (*New Guinea: What I Did and What I Saw*, 1880) his observations of and experiences with the Roro, mainly on Yule Island, in 1875. His remarks on persons and personal relationships are especially interesting. We then come to one of a line of scholars—members of the Sacred Heart Mission in Papua who have contributed much to our knowledge of the languages and peoples of the districts in which they have worked, willingly and wholeheartedly assisting anthropologists and linguists. Joseph Guis, M.S.C., wrote *La Vie des Papous*, dealing with the Mekeo, Roro and Pokao, on the basis of work in the district and with natives from it during 1894-97. After Seligman came R. W. Williamson with an account of "Some Unrecorded Customs of the Mekeo People", observed by him in 1910. Nothing else is available, but the Sacred Heart Mission has at Yule

Island an excellent collection of Roro folk-lore, which should be published.

Inland neighbours of both the Roro and Mekeo are the Kuni, about whom some contributions have appeared in *Anthropos*: Fr. Eschlimann (1911) on the child in Kuni Society, and Fr. Egidi, myths and legends. Williamson (*Mafulu*, index) also refers frequently to the Kuni and the Kovio people in behind the Mekeo; little has been reported, nor has any research been done amongst the Kabadi on the east of the Pokao. Indeed, the last two are diminishing rapidly. As for the other south-western tribes of the Central Division, their populations seem to be somewhere about 5,000 each, the Mekeo being given as 4,000 in the 1934-5 census.

The Mekeo are coming more and more in contact with non-native influences, other than the Mission, particularly through visits to Port Moresby, and through agricultural developments sponsored by the Administration. This requires a forward move in education and also a sociological study of their society and culture, of their child-adult relations, and of their attitudes to white culture in general and to missions in particular.[1] This is an opportunity for a mission anthropologist. Fortunately, not only for the Mekeo, but also for tribes further in the interior, the Mission with its increasing knowledge of the languages is initially well-equipped to make the necessary research, on which both mission progress and native well-being is best founded. The history of the Sacred Heart Mission shows it usually has one or more members well endowed for such specialized work, and of course, training in field-research method is available.

In the interior mountainous region north of the Mekeo and Kuni, apart from administrative patrols, the continued process of exploring and making contact with its Papuan dwellers has been mainly the concern of this Mission. Some idea of this can be gained from André Dupeyrat's *Papouasie*. Further, the only methodical work on an inland group, Williamson's *Mafulu* would have been of much less value without the help of missionaries. Nothing else has been published about this tribe, also known as the Fuyuge, apart from some notes in *Papua Reports*. No research has been done amongst the Ononghe, who speak a related language, or a dialect, of their western neighbour, the Mafulu, nor amongst the Tauata or Apekove (except for an article by

[1]A preliminary study has been made; C. S. Belshaw: "Recent History of Mekeo Society". *Oceania*, Vol. XXII, No. 1, 1951, pp. 1-23.

Fr. Egidi), and the tribes in the north-west. E. W. P. Chinnery wrote a few notes on the Kuefa Tribe on the north of Mt. Yule, and referred to other tribes beyond this one, including the Kunimaipa-linguistic area, which extends to the head of the Waria (a New Guinea river).

This last-named area, into which both Roman Catholic and London Missionary Society (from the Toaripi country) missions are extending, and which was for so long undisturbed in its mountain fastness, should be considered for research. The process of culture-change amongst the Kunimaipa could then be studied from time to time in its various stages.

I suggest, however, that this whole western interior should be made the subject of an anthropological and census survey, so as to determine the locations and numbers of the peoples there, their possible economic improvement, their likely movements, and a place or places for intensive research. In this survey, a mission anthropologist, or else a visiting anthropologist, and an experienced and senior administrative officer should work together for some months. In any case the Mission, which knows the region so well, should be represented.

The population of this interior is not satisfactorily known, but it runs into thousands, and is considered by an officer well experienced in the district to exceed 25,000. For example, from Ononghe to the Mt. Turu tribes, west of the Kunimaipa, and including the Goilala, reckoning four to a house, the number is 6,250.

This inland area is very rough country, with a cold climate at a usual living height of 6,000 feet. Inquiry is needed to devise satisfactory means of improving the food-supply where salt, oils and meat are deficient. There is little hunting. Nut-bearing trees and pigs and goats could probably be introduced, but the country is too rugged for cattle. Good use could be made of goat skins. The spread of literacy, which is usually necessary if improvements in diet and ways of life are to be established, will raise its own wants. These will need some money for satisfaction. The possibility of growing tea, Arabian coffee of high quality, quinine and nuts for sale should be considered. The roughness of the country precludes the export of timber.

Such are matters to be borne in mind by the survey I suggest.

References

L. M. d'Albertis: *New Guinea: What I Did and What I Saw*, Vol. I, 1880, pp. 243-398.
C. G. Seligman: *The Melanesians of British New Guinea*, 1910, pp. 195-374.
J. Guis, M.S.C.: *La Vie des Papous*, 1936, pp. 1-238.

F. R. Barton, C.M.G.: "Children's Games in Br. New Guinea". *J.A.I.* Vol. 38, 1908, pp. 259-79.

R. W. Williamson: "Some Unrecorded Customs of the Mekeo People, Br. New Guinea". *J.R.A.I.*, Vol. 43, 1913, pp. 268-90.

H. Eschlimann (Rev.): "L'Enfant chez les Kuni" (Nouvelle Guinée Anglaise). *Anthropos,* Vol. 6, 1911, pp. 260-75.

V. M. Egidi (Rev.): "Mythes et légendes des Kuni, Br. New Guinea". *Anthropos,* Vol. 8, 1913, pp. 978-1009, Vol. 9, 1914, pp. 81-97, 392-404.

R. W. Williamson: *The Mafulu: Mountain People of British New Guinea,* 1912, pp. 1-364. Introduction by A. C. Haddon.

V. M. Egidi: "La tribu di Tanata". *Anthropos,* Vol. 2, 1907, pp. 675-81; 1009-21.

E. W. P. Chinnery: "Notes on Tribes in Vicinity of Mt. Yule, Chapman, Strong and St. Mary". *Papua Report,* 1916-17, pp. 59-63.

André Dupeyrat: *Papouasie,* 1935.

S. H. Ray: "The Language of the Central Division of Papua". *J.R.A.I.*, Vol. 59, 1929, pp. 65-96.

Central Division—Eastern Half

The pioneer exploration of this area, and contact with its natives, was in the hands of London Missionary Society missionaries, and this mission is still responsible for most missionary and education work in the Division east of Port Moresby. Chalmers gives us some of the first glimpses we get of the Motu, Koita, Koiari, Sinaugoro and other tribes.

The Koita

Although the wide use of the Motu language by the Mission and the wider use of pidgin-Motu by the Administration gives the impression that the Motu is a large tribe, this is not so. The Motu, like other coastal groups east of Cape Possession, are Melanesian intruders. The Motu pushed back and to some extent mingled with the Koita, a Papuan people. The early missionary writers, like W. Y. Turner (1878) and W. G. Lawes (1879) distinguished the two from each other and from the Koiari on their immediate north. Professor Seligman gave a separate section to the aboriginal Koita, but for years past they have been expected to lose their identity in the general Motu environment, their speech not being provided for in missionary and educational activity.

I am not surprised to read in Dr. Capell's 1947 Report on his "Linguistic Investigation in Papua", that the Koita are not satisfied at being overlooked in this way. They want to see their language in print and in some cases, to see their history recorded. Ahuia Ova, a Koita "chief", a helper of Haddon, Seligman and Williams, was most anxious that the latter should be done, and to help in the project. Such an opportunity, of course, should not be lost. It is not only a matter of recording all facts for later scientific analysis, but the recording of history, language and culture as a means of preserving continuity with the past, building up pride in one's own tribe's or people's achievements and so providing a psychological attitude of well-being and self-confidence for the future.

Two samples of Ahuia Ova's work have been published, one by the Rev. J. B. Clark: "Motu Feasts and Dances", *Papua Report*, 1922-23, pp. 37-40, and the other by F. E. Williams: "The Reminiscences of Ahuia Ova", *J.R.A.I.*, Vol. 69, 1939, pp. 11-45.

There may not be many Koita—Roku had 115 inhabitants during my visit in 1946—and I passed two other Koita villages. But they were alive to all post-war changes, and whether a community be small or large, especially when it is at the geographical centre of a Territory, a special effort is worth while to forestall a feeling of being slighted.

The Koiari

The Koita are also of interest because of their relationship in language and common origin with the inland Koiari. These independent people, because of their independent attitude and because of the difficult nature of their country, have been a good deal neglected except for some prohibitions and very little missionary work, both effective only in the nearer districts. The main fact known about them was their definite decrease in numbers, of which the suppression of their homicidal cult with its effect on marriage was definitely a contributing factor. My inquiries in 1946 convinced me that a thorough sociological study of these people was required, to be followed, I hoped, by some positive welfare measures. No country can afford merely to watch the passing of an independent community or tribe—a tribe which despises the dwellers near the town who allow so much to be done for them. The original purpose for Dr. Capell's visit in early 1947 was to lay a basis for this research by studying the Koiari from a linguistic and socio-linguistic point of view. I still recommend that the Koiari be selected for a well-rounded project of anthropological research. There is a problem of depopulation and of development to be solved.

Apart from the references in Government reports and in missionaries' articles and books, the only anthropological study of any aspect of Koiari culture is F. E. Williams' study (1932) of Koiari plant emblems in relation to kinship, marriage, and inheritance.

The Motu

To return to the Koita, both they and the Motu were the objects of statistical attention in the second decade of the century when much interest was being taken in population problems—and rightly so. Both tribes were represented in the three Port Moresby villages— Hanuabada, Tanobada and Elavala, and were therefore definitely exposed to contact. It was found that from 1916 to 1919 they were "weathering the storm"; the Koita showing a yearly average increase of 7.1, and the Motu, 14.1, while the total population of the three villages increased from 1,626 in 1915 to 1,744 in 1920, and births continued to exceed deaths during the pre-war years.

As for the Motu, in addition to missionary references already given, and Seligman, there is a special chapter (VIII) in the latter by Captain Barton on the Motuans' trading expeditions, or *hiri*, in their lakatoi. J. T. O'Malley recorded in 1912 a native's own version of sorcery and various customs, translated from Motu. Apart from these references there is little else worth while. The Motu, like several other tribes, are mentioned in general articles on different aspects of Papuan culture, such as string figures (Rosser and Hornell) and tattooing (Captain Barton).

It is therefore good to know that Dr. C. S. Belshaw, on an Australian National University Fellowship, plans to make a socio-economic study of the Port Moresby villages, now adjacent and called collectively Hanuabada. This is a much needed type of research project.[1]

As for the rest of the Central Division, no real research has been carried out. The London Missionary Society missionaries have worked for years amongst the tribes, especially along the coast, such as the Sinangolo and the Hula, but there are also some inland tribes, the Seramina, Kokila and Kwale. The Hula expeditions to Port Moresby were known, but not studied as an institution.[2] Seligman recorded a few pages on the medicine, surgery and midwifery of the Sinangolo.

The population of the Rigo Sub-administrative District was about 7,000 in 1928, but as at present constituted is given by one officer as 18,000, while the central or Moresby Sub-District numbers about 14,000.

[1]This work is now completed.—A. P. E., November, 1952.
[2]Dr. Belshaw made a preliminary study in 1951: "Port Moresby Canoe Traders". *Oceania*, Vol. XXIII, No. 1, 1952, pp. 26-39.

References

W. Y. Turner (Rev.): "The Ethnology of the Motu". *J.A.I.*, Vol. 7, 1878, pp. 470-97.

W. G. Lawes: "Ethnological Notes on the Motu, Koitapu and Koiari Tribes of New Guinea". *J.A.I.*, Vol. VIII, 1879, pp. 369-76.

C. G. Seligman: op. cit. (1910) pp. 41-194.

J. T. O'Malley: "Native Affairs:—Natives' own version of Sorcery etc. translated from Motuan". *Papua Report*, 1911-12, pp. 98-105.

Ahuia Ova: "Motu Feasts and Dances". *Papua Report*, 1922-3, pp. 37-40. Trans. by Rev. J. B. Clark.

F. E. Williams: "The Reminiscences of Ahuia Ova". *J.R.A.I.*, Vol. 69, 1939, pp. 11-45.

F. E. Williams: "Sex Affiliation and its Implications". *J.R.A.I.*, Vol. 62, 1932, pp. 51-81.

W. E. Rosser & J. Hornell: "String Figures from Br. New Guinea". *J.R.A.I.*, Vol. 62, 1932, pp. 39-50.

F. R. Barton: "Tattooing in S.E. New Guinea". *J.R.A.I.*, Vol. 48, 1918, pp. 22-79.

C. G. Seligman: "The Medicine, Surgery and Midwifery of the Sinangolo". *J.A.I.*, Vol. 32, 1902, pp. 297-305.

5. THE EAST–CENTRAL SUB–DIVISION AND EASTERN DIVISION

I am treating the East-Central Sub-Division (now in the Central Division) along with the Eastern Division, in which it was until recently included.

The Mainland District

Once again, our early information, incidental in character, comes from missionaries and explorers, and from official reports. By the turn of the century, as a result of London Missionary Society work and of administrative policy, the natives of the Division were becoming friendlily disposed towards Europeans, though the apathy of the natives in areas of much contact was regarded as the greatest obstacle to their progress. With this went an official warning in 1899 not to assume too readily that because the native sometimes imitates Europeans or adapts himself for a time to their ways, he is convinced of the superiority of these ways and intends to follow them.

Actually, the native is making what he regards as a necessary adaptation to the European, his demands and idiosyncrasies, in the interests of his own preservation and, if possible, to his own benefit. All research into culture-contact situations must take stock of this principle of adaptation. My own inquiries and information in and regarding both Papua, New Guinea and Aboriginal Australia, have revealed its operation.

This implies a warning against too hasty complete substitution of English for the native language and of European doctrines, activities and ways of life for the indigenous culture. There is always the danger of the "double life" adaptation, which is not in the best interests of personal integration and, therefore, of educational aims; alternatively, in spite of the apparent success of the substitution method, there is the likelihood either of a "Vailala" type of cult-madness or an endeavour to return to and revive the old ways in some garbled form. This is likely as soon as a break in supervision or a lapse in the behaviour of leaders occurs, or disappointment arises with the material, physical or social results of the substituted way of life and thought.

This is to the point here, because one of the few anthropological projects undertaken in this Division was concerned with a people, the Keveri, whose way of life had been completely divorced from the past, as is the inevitable practical result of the policy of the highly commendable, industrious and Christian Mission, the Kwato—at Abau. This investigation was made in early 1940 by that very practical, intensely human and experienced anthropologist, F. E. Williams. Earlier references to the Keveri and other groups in the District can be seen in official reports, including W. R. Humphries, "The Keveri Valley", 1923.

The most studied group in the mainland part of the Division is the Mailu, whose country extended along the coast from Cape Rodney to the middle of Orangerie Bay, Amazon Bay being their main centre. Malinowski's field-work in 1914 and missionary Saville's sound book, In Unknown New Guinea, 1926, written under the former's influence, provide an adequate understanding of this people. The mission station has now been moved from the island of Mailu to the mainland. Field-work might well be carried out there, on the basis of the earlier researches, for the purpose of revealing the extent of changes caused by mission, government, labour and war. In the final selection of tribes for this type of research project, the Mailu should be considered.

The Abau-Mailu population figures are about 10,000.

Further east, for the Suau in the south and the Tawala on Milne Bay, W. E. Armstrong, Assistant Government Anthropologist, gathered some information ("Report on Suau-Tawala", Papua Report, 1920-21, and later, 1926 and 1932); and F. E. Williams made a special study of depopulation in the Suau district ("Depopulation of the Suau District", Anthropology Report, No. 13). This was a "sample" study, for in the 1920's the whole Eastern Division was decreasing; the excess of deaths over births in 1924-6 being 508; this unsatisfactory condition was again reported in 1934, with the exception of the Abau district, and it still prevails. This Suau depopulation problem requires further study.

As a control, there is the Keveri Valley in the hinterland, whose population is reported to be increasing.

Dr. Capell recommends Suau as a suitable "union" language for the eastern tip of the mainland, to be used in vernacular teaching. If this course be adopted, we will have an added reason to carry out further research into the culture of the district, so as to have a full understanding of the language.

References

S. H. Ray: "Comparative Notes in Massim and other Languages of Eastern Papua". *J.R.A.I.*, 1911, pp. 397-405.

F. E. Williams: "Mission Influence Amongst the Keveri of S.E. Papua". *Oceania*, Vol. XV, No. 2, 1944, pp. 89-142.

B. Malinowski: "The Natives of Mailu": Preliminary Results of the Robert Mond Research Work in British New Guinea. *Royal Society of South Australia*, 1915, Vol. 39, pp. 494-706.

W. J. V. Saville: *In Unknown New Guinea*, 1926, pp. 1-316. (Introduction by B. Malinowski.)

W. E. Armstrong: "Report on Suau-Tawala". *Papua Report* 1920-21, pp. 32-45.

F. E. Williams: "Depopulation of the Suau District". *Anthropology Report* No. 13.

C. G. Seligman: op. cit. pp. 376-659 for the Wagawaga and Bartle Bay district on the mainland, and for the island of Tubetube.

W. E. Armstrong: Suau Folk-tales (in Suau); Typescript.

Eastern Division—Insular District

The harvest is great, but the labourers few, has ever been, and still is, the blunt anthropological fact. It is true on the mainland, but in the islands—so numerous—it seems truer still, if that is possible. The selection of sample islands is difficult, and to study the lot with their different languages and customs is impossible. The administrator must keep in contact with certain aspects of behaviour in all his demesne. Missionaries, in the zeal of their vocation, cannot rest until they have worked on all the islands, never mind how many tongues they must learn. But the anthropologist! He must be selective.

Seligman grouped the Papuo-Melanesians of the eastern islands of Papua into two main types, the northern and the southern Massim. Malinowski went further and sub-divided these again, but more important, he was able to determine the factor which linked most of these island groups in a degree of unity; this is the circular inter-trading and exchange system of the Kula. It is discussed in the first chapter ("The Country and Inhabitants of the Kula District") of that great gem of anthropological literature, *Argonauts of the Western Pacific*, 1922. Actually, the Kula is the theme of this book, and also forms an important section of Dr. Fortune's report on Dobu.

Many references to this island area (the Massim) appear in the *Papua Reports* right down the years, but the first anthropological investigation was made by Seligman. He wrote on Tubetube and Bartle Bay. During the first half of 1950 Dr. C. S. Belshaw studied culture-change at Wagawaga (in Milne Bay) and at Ware (Teste), south-east of Samarai. His visit was most timely, especially in the former case. The old culture has gone, but the people do not understand the practical consequences of their urge for modernity. With regard to the Ware, Dr. Belshaw has shown that, while outside the Kula ring, the islanders have their own trade and ceremonial relationships with Misima and with the mainland.

In 1922 W. E. Armstrong reported briefly on the D'Entrecasteaux and Engineer Groups, Basilaki and as far east as Sudest and Rossel in the South-East Division. Actually, the D'Entrecasteaux group has been best studied. For Normanby there is the interesting material from Dr. Roheim in *Oceania*, which gives a good insight into native beliefs. For the Dobuans we have a good deal of material. Dobuan language and cultural influence extend to the north of Normanby and the eastern tip of the Fergusson Islands also, and according to the 1932 census included 7,000 persons. W. E. Bromilow's articles in 1909 and 1911 and his *Twenty Years among Primitive Papuans*, 1929, are a necessary background to Dr. Fortune's *Sorcerers of Dobu*, 1932. Between them they leave little to be gathered about the past. Dr. Fortune worked on Tewara Island, east of Fergusson.

For Goodenough Island and North Fergusson, Jenness and Ballantyne (1920 and 1926-7) provide a succinct account of the culture and social structure, and preserve some of the folk-tales. They are concerned mainly with the Bwaidoga-speaking group, which numbered 8,600 in 1932. Normanby, Fergusson and Goodenough and the smaller associated islands have a population of about 30,000. Fergusson alone has about 12,000. In addition to Dobuan at the eastern end, there are several other dialects or languages on the Island. At present, Dr. W. E. Smythe is carrying out a medical project connected with population problems, which demands prior linguistic research amongst the 916 Kukuja-speaking people at Giria on the south of the Island. He reports four languages related to the Kukuja: one spoken in the Salakahadi valley in the interior; the Morima on the south coast; a third on the north-east tip of the Island and the Kalokalo towards the north-west. There are possibly other languages or dialects also.

Dr. Smythe urges that the selected regional language should not possess the glottal stop, for the Kukuja find it insuperable.

Depopulation has not yet been established for the Island, but in the district being studied masculinity is high. Consequently the absence of men at work does not affect the population. Whether the birth-rate is being consciously retarded, or whether other factors are operating, has yet to be determined. I suggest that an experienced woman anthropologist, working amongst the women, as well as studying the general social and cultural set-up, could give great help in this piece of research. So far, in the islands, not nearly enough work has been done with the women concerning their side of life, both intimate and less private. But without their co-operation we cannot obtain full understanding.

Mission Anthropologist: Apart from this special problem project, there is opportunity for research into parts of these islands which have not yet been studied, and also into the present social and cultural condition, but there does not seem to be any urgency. A general survey, however, would be to the point. The Methodist Mission would be helping its own plans and also the natives' progress if it saw that one of its members was well trained in anthropology, given *two* years at Sydney University for this purpose, and then set aside to specialize in anthropological research, stock-taking and advisory work for the Mission.

References

C. G. Seligman: op. cit. pp. 376-659 for Tubetube, Wagawaga and Bartle Bay (Wedau etc.).

W. E. Armstrong: "Report on Anthropology of S. Eastern Division (excluding Woodlark Island), Engineer Group, Basilaki, East Cape, Normanby Island (Sth. Coast), Fergusson Island (Morima)". *Papua Report*, 1921-22, pp. 26-36.

G. Roheim: "Witches of Normanby Island". *Oceania*, Vol. XVIII, No. 4, 1948, pp. 279-309.

G. Roheim: "Yaboaine, a War God of Normanby Island". *Oceania*, Vol. XVI, No. 3, 1946, pp. 210-34; Vol. XVI, No. 4, 1946, pp. 319-37.

W. E. Bromilow (Rev.): "Some Manners and Customs of the Dobuans of S. E. Papua". *Australian Association for the Advancement of Science*, Vol. XII, Brisbane, 1909, pp. 470-85.

W. E. Bromilow: "Dobuan (Papua) Beliefs and Folk-lore". *Australian Association for the Advancement of Science*, Vol. XIII, Sydney, 1911, pp. 413-26.

W. E. Bromilow: *Twenty Years among Primitive Papuans*, 1929, pp. 1-316.

R. F. Fortune: *Sorcerers of Dobu*, 1932, pp. 1-306. (Introduction by B. Malinowski.)

D. Jenness & (Rev.) A. Ballantyne: *The Northern D'Entrecasteaux*, 1920, pp. 1-216. (Preface by R. R. Marett.)

D. Jenness: "Papuan Cat's Cradles". *J.R.A.I.*, Vol. 50, 1920, pp. 299-326.

D. Jenness & A. Ballantyne: "Language Mythology and Songs of Bwaidoga". *Polynesian Society Journal*, Vol. 35, 1926, pp. 290-314. Vol. 36, 1927, pp. 48-71 and 145-79.

O. J. Atkinson: "Description of the Gwedi Gwedi People". *Papua Report*, 1921-22, pp. 152-4.

S. H. Ray: "Languages of the Eastern and South-Eastern Divisions of Papua". *J.R.A.I.*, Vol. 68, 1938, pp. 153-208.

6. SOUTH-EASTERN DIVISION

Proceeding from the D'Entrecasteaux north, we come to the Trobriand Islands, the most and best studied society in the whole region.
Malinowski alone published over 2,100 pages directly on it. In earlier
days and later, these Islands received much notice in the Annual
Reports mainly because the population seemed to be decreasing.
This was reported for 1906-7, venereal diseases coming in for a share
of the blame. The decrease was reported to be still continuing throughout 1920-26, though opinions varied as to the extent. The birth rate
was too low. Influenza wrought havoc. But the mourning custom of
Kavalua, which meant that a widow practically starved herself and
her baby if she had one, was also blamed by R. L. Bellamy (Resident
Magistrate). Mr. Leo Austen, however, in 1934 showed that there were
few if any signs of depopulation. As far back as 1906-7 Mr. Bellamy
gave the population as 8,000. The census for 1932 gave it as 8,600.

A more interesting aspect was touched upon in the Annual Reports.
In 1898-99 the principal chief of the archipelago, after a long period
of refusal, allowed the Methodist Mission to establish a station in his
own village, in the Kiriwina district. In the following year it is reported
that there.was a rising and the old chief, Enamakala, was overthrown,
his village burned and his gardens pillaged and destroyed. There is no
suggestion of relating the two as cause and effect.

The Trobrianders, however, survived the revolution, and also the
work of the Methodist Mission and later of the Roman Catholic
Mission. Indeed, through these agencies, they have become to a great
extent literate; and although there have been some changes in their
culture, the complete breakdown referred to in an early report has
not occurred. Keeping to themselves except when moving on the
business of the Kula trading voyages, they have shown little interest
in signing on for work which would take them from their own
region, and have always regarded their own cultural and social affairs
as claiming their attention in preference to outside affairs. The Trobrianders, therefore, for this reason and also because of wise administration, are a people whose progress as a community is still feasible.

In addition to Malinowski's research we have R. L. Bellamy's short
report (1907) on the social organization, and a useful series of articles by
Mr. Leo Austen (Assistant Resident Magistrate) 1934-1945, and two
articles on Trobriand songs by Fr. Baldwin.

Finally, in 1950, Mr. H. A. Powell, as part of his post-graduate work for the London University Ph.D., began a study of the present culture-contact position in the Trobriands.[1] This, of course, fits in with the general principle that all areas which have been well studied ten or more years ago should be re-studied as soon as possible. He returned from the field in 1951.

No anthropological research has been done in the rest of this Division except on Rossel Island or Yule in the far south-east. For this, an isolated Papuan-speaking island with a population of about 1,500, W. E. Armstrong published an excellent study of the social organization and its unique form of currency. This was based on field-work in 1921. Rossel is a very isolated island and difficult to approach. The Roman Catholic Mission from Basilaki visits the Island but has no resident missionary. The language is difficult and has not yet been mastered. Interesting as the culture is, there is no particular reason for recommending research there at present. It would, however, be interesting to know whether the shell currency described by Armstrong is still functioning.

Between the Trobriands and Rossel are several groups, some of which have been visited by anthropologists, though not studied; nor does there appear to be any demand for intensive research on them. Their populations are for the most part small: the Marshall Bennett Group with about 500, linguistically related to Kiriwina, Woodlark (Murua)—about 700 or so—a community which has had much experience of white men over a long period, and which, like the Laughlin (Nada) of 200 souls, is related by language and the Kula to the Trobriands; and south-west of Woodlark, the Tokena (about 80) and Egum (not known). South-east are Misima (2,300), Panauati (600), Calvados (400) and Sudest (1900).

References

R. L. Bellamy: "Notes on the Customs of the Trobriand Islander". *Annual Report,* Papua, 1906-7, pp. 63-6.

C. G. Seligman: op. cit. pp. 660-753 for Trobriands, Marshall Bennetts and Murua.

B. Malinowski: "The Spirits of the Dead in the Trobriand Islands", *J.R.A.I.,* Vol. 46, 1916, pp. 353-431.

B. Malinowski: *Argonauts of the Western Pacific,* 1922, pp. 1-519. (Introduction by J. G. Frazer.)

B. Malinowski: "Forschungen in einer mutter-rechtlichen Gemeinde". *Zeitschrift für Volkspsychologie & Soziologie,* Vol. I, 1925, pp. 45-53, 278-84.

B. Malinowski: *Crime and Custom in Savage Society,* 1926, pp. 1-129.

B. Malinowski: *Myth in Primitive Psychology,* 1926, pp. 1-128.

[1] This work is now completed.—A. P. E., November 1952.

B. Malinowski: "Lunar and Seasonal Calendar in the Trobriands". *J.R.A.I.*, Vol. 57, 1927, pp. 203-15.

B. Malinowski: *Sexual Life of Savages*, 1929, pp. 1-480.

B. Malinowski: *Coral Gardens and Their Magic*, Vols. I and II, 1935. Vol. 1: pp. 1-385. Vol. II: pp. 1-342.

L. Austen: "Procreation Among the Trobriand Islanders". *Oceania*, Vol. V, No. 1. 1934, pp. 202-14.

L. Austen: "The Seasonal Gardening Calendar of Kiriwina, Trobriand Islands". *Oceania*, Vol. IX, No. 3, 1939, pp. 237-54.

L. Austen: "Megalithic Structures in the Trobriand Islands". *Oceania*, Vol. X, No. 1, 1939, pp. 30-54.

L. Austen: "Cultural Changes in Kiriwina". *Oceania*, Vol. XVI, No. 1, 1945, pp. 15-21.

L. Austen: "Native Handicrafts in the Trobriand Islands". *Mankind*, Vol. 3, No. 7, April 1945, pp. 193-99.

B. Baldwin: "Usituma! Song of Heaven". *Oceania*, Vol. XV, No. 3, 1945, pp. 201-39.

B. Baldwin: Kadaguwai: Songs of the Trobriand Sunset Isles". *Oceania*, Vol. XX, No. 4, 1950, pp. 263-85.

W. E. Armstrong: *Rossel Island*, 1928, pp. 1-274.

C. G. Seligman: *The Melanesians of Br. New Guinea*, 1910, pp. 754.

L. N. Brown: "The Island of Misima". *Papua Report*, 1922-23, pp. 21-22.

7. THE NORTH-EASTERN AND NORTHERN DIVISIONS

Crossing back to the Papuan mainland at the eastern end of the North-Eastern Division, we find ourselves in the Anglican Mission area; indeed, this extends throughout the North-Eastern and Northern Divisions and includes a small coastal portion of the mainland of the Eastern Division. Some of the early missionaries, particularly the Rev. Copland King, did valuable linguistic work; he produced dictionaries and grammars of Wedau (1901) and Binandere (1927). Sangara is being studied and used. Of the social structure and the culture of the peoples in these Divisions, there are none but superficial observations available, except for the Orokaiva in the Binandere language area in the north, in the Mambare district, thanks principally to F. E. Williams' *Orokaiva Magic*, 1928, *Orokaiva Society*, 1930, and an earlier article, 1925. Dr. Williams worked mainly at Opi on the Upper Opi River. Mr. W. Beaver, too, wrote briefly in the Annual Reports on these people. We therefore have basic knowledge for the Orokaiva, which would provide a background for sociological research into the present condition of the society and of its cultural adjustment.

When, however, this intensive project is undertaken, I recommend that the same anthropologist remain sufficiently long to survey the two divisions—unless a second scientist can be obtained to cover part of the ground—to make a study of the social and cultural integration of, at least, the principal communities. He should also study the attitudes of the people, especially the younger adults, to the "new order" which has come upon them through miners, traders and planters, administration and the Mission, and the extent to which the war, with its Japanese invasion and later Allied "invasion" of their country, has affected their outlook and attitudes. Many of the men of these Divisions served in the Papuan Infantry Battalion, in labour gangs and as carriers. Some of the young men from the region whom I met in 1946 were somewhat critical of what had been done for them and their womenfolk in pre-war days. They were not desirous of being forever "hewers of wood and drawers of water", not even in the interest of religion.

The large Orokaiva group (numbered in 1950 at 15,000) around Higaturu, the Upper Kumusi and the Opi Rivers, as well as the coastal people of the Buna-Gona areas, are of importance in this connexion. A people of independent character, and reported to be difficult—which seems on the spot to mean reserved and thoughtful—the Orokaiva do not take us at face value. Coming into a money economy, which they do not sufficiently understand, they suspect this and doubt that, with regard to money in the bank, intestate estates and payment for war damages, but fortunately they are willing to argue with officers they know. It looks as though these people would develop best along lines of community and co-operative enterprise rather than in employment. This, like their understanding of our money economy, will depend on education and literacy. This in turn, will depend on the Mission being able to step up its education programme and standard, and on the Education Department, which now has only one school in these Divisions, at Kokoda, being in a position to do much more. This education, however, should, I think, include literacy in Orokaiva, both as an acknowledgement of the tribal heritage, and as a sound preliminary to literacy in English. The Mission too, should also develop the use of the language in its Churches as well as in schools. The recent example of the Rev. (now Bishop) D. Hand in this regard should be followed.

Returning to the coast, we remember that the Rev. Copland King reported the Baigona Cult from the Mambare in the 1911-12 Annual Report, and that Chinnery and Haddon wrote in 1917 not only of this Cult, but also of the Kava-Kava and the Kekesi from near the same place, two of which cults spread down the coast. There was also the "prophet of Milne Bay". In other words, whatever the cause, the psychological conditions or their effects were not satisfactory or integrating. There may be no similar reaction, or reaction to contact, if any, may take some other form; but a knowledge of attitudes would be worth while.

When I was in the district in 1950, two missionaries of long experience in the coastal district of the Northern Division expressed the view that the co-operative movement which is developing strongly there is a sublimation of the Taro Cult. It is a spontaneous movement, and makes use of such features of the social structure as age grades and kinship. A study of this development might throw light on the way in which the natives there blend the old and the new.

From the point of view of language it seems that half the coast of the North-Eastern and almost all the coast of the Northern Division can be served by Binandere, even in the case of the varying dialects spoken around Collingwood Bay, across the Tufi Peninsula and around Dyke Acland Bay to Emo: such as the Ubiri, Maisin, Korafi, Mokurewa, Okeina and Buruga. These and related, and sometimes quite isolated dialects, are spoken by about 5,000 people. At Oro Bay we pass to the Motu speakers and so on to Binandere proper which takes us to the border of Papua. It seemed to me, while passing through the region, that, being equipped with Binandere, and gaining a knowledge of Kworapi, passing into Motu, a field-worker could make a thorough sociological survey and study of this important coastal region.

Apart from Dr. Williams' books on the Orokaiva, there is little published material for these Divisions. The Rev. A. K. Chignell's *An Outpost in Papua*, 1915, is of interest for the Wanigela district, though it gives no insight into the real life of the people, for as he said of ceremonial aspects of the culture, which impinged on mission work, he was "too ignorant of the whole matter to give any description of the details, or of their significance", but still any features considered objectionable were dispensed with in deference to the missionary's wishes. Bishop Newton's *In Far New Guinea* gives information over a wider area. C. A. W. Monckton's *Some Experiences of a New Guinea Resident Magistrate* (Volume II) gives a picture of the contact position in his day.

We have also a few notes for the Baniara and Cape Nelson districts, and for further north, contributions by Chinnery and Beaver on initiation amongst the Koko, in the Yodda Valley, and on movements of the tribes of the Mambare region.

Highlands of the Northern and North-Eastern Division

On the highlands of these Divisions and in adjacent parts of the Central Division there are tribes which have not been studied at all, and which would repay research. These include the Chirima (Tsirime) Valley natives near Mt. Albert-Edward, who are on the head-waters of the Mambare. The Sacred Heart Mission is operating among them. South-east are the Wowonga of the Mt. Obree district—"a people with long hair and pigtails", whose language and culture extends into the Upper Kumusi. They could be approached from Rigo. One group of these could be worked with from the heads of the Kemp-welch River, and another group approached from the south of Mt. Obree.

In between the Chirima and the Wowonga is the Kokoda group. The field-worker could start with the Biaga (Huga) and work towards the Koiari and so to Port Moresby. This district is noted for its songs.

References

W. Beaver: "Description of the life of the Orokaiva People". *Papua Report*, 1914-15, pp. 48-51.

W. Beaver: "Notes on the Homicidal Emblems among the Orokaiva". *Papua Report*, 1918-19, pp. 96-9.

F. E. Williams: "Plant Emblems among the Orokaiva". *J.R.A.I.*, Vol. 55, 1925, pp. 405-24.

F. E. Williams: *Orokaiva Magic*, 1928, pp. 1-229. (Foreword by R. R. Marett).

F. E. Williams: *Orokaiva Society*, 1930, pp. 1-341. (Introduction by Sir Hubert Murray).

(Rev.) Copland King: "The Baigona Cult". *Papua Report*, 1911-12, pp. 154-5.

E. W. P. Chinnery: and A. C. Haddon: "Five New Religious Cults in British New Guinea". *Hibbert Journal*, Vol. XV, No. 3, 1917, pp. 448-63.

L. A. Flint: "Practice of Spiritualism among the Mukawa Natives". *Papua Report*, 1919-20, pp. 111-12.

L. A. Flint: "Burial Customs of the Desi Tribe". *Papua Report*, 1919-20, pp. 112-13.

A. Liston-Blyth: "Notes on Native Customs in the Baniara District (N.E.D.), Papua". *J.R.A.I.*, Vol. 53, 1923, pp. 467-71.

(Dr.) Rudolph Pöch: "Einige bemerkenswerte Ethnologica aus Neu-Guinea". *Mitteilungen der Anthropologischen Gesellschaft in Wien*, Vol. 37, 1907, pp. 57-71; also "Nachtrage zur Einige bemerkenswerte Ethnologica aus Neu-Guinea", op. cit. p. 125.

E. W. P. Chinnery and W. Beaver: "Notes on the Initiation Ceremonies of the Koko, Papua". *J.R.A.I.*, Vol. 45, 1915, pp. 69-78.

E. W. P. Chinnery and W. N. Beaver: "The Movements of the Tribes of the Mambare Division of Northern Papua". *Papua Report*, 1914-15, pp. 158-61. (With language chart of the Northern Districts of Papua and comparative table of languages, pp. 161-67).

7

TRUST TERRITORY OF NEW GUINEA

ANTHROPOLOGICAL research expeditions into Papua have been comparatively few: Landtman, Seligman, Malinowski (two areas), Humphries, Jenness, Fortune and Williams. Were it not for Dr. Williams' five main fields of work and others in which he carried out shorter and specific inquiries, the total record would seem slight, in spite of Malinowski's very great contribution. Missionaries' records of anthropological material, too, are few in number: books by J. H. Holmes and W. J. Saville, and occasional articles in scientific journals. Passing into the Trust Territory of New Guinea, however, we find that it has been a very attractive territory—anthropologically speaking. In the German days, natural historians were interested in it, many of whom provided useful accounts of the native peoples. Missionaries, both Lutheran and Roman Catholic, observed, studied and recorded various aspects of the cultures, and did so in scholarly fashion. In some cases they collaborated with anthropologists or ethnologists in Germany or Austria. Parkinson, though neither scientist nor missionary, provided what has become a classic work on the region—his *Dreissig Jahre in der Südsee.*

With regard to research by anthropological specialists, particularly since the first World War, the Territory exerted very widespread attraction in England, America and Germany as well as in Australia. The Australian National Research Council, thanks to grants from the Rockefeller Foundation, planned research in the Territory, sending its own field-workers out, and collaborating with, and assisting, those from other countries—Thurnwald (who had been out in earlier years as well) and Mrs. Thurnwald, Bateson, Mead, Fortune, Bell, Todd, Powdermaker, Wedgwood, Groves, Hogbin, S. W. Reed, Whiting, Oliver, Kaberry and Chinnery (Government Anthropologist and Director of District Services); and since the second World War, K. E. Read, Hogbin and Lawrence. Six of these have worked in two fields. Of course, the area, population and variety of cultures are greater than in the case of Papua, but certainly the record gives the impression of a very real and almost concerted attempt being made

64

to know and understand the people. In pre-1914 years, this was part of the German trait of thoroughness. Since 1921, it can be correlated with the Mandate status of the Territory. The Australian Government accepted the view of the Pan-Pacific Science Congress of 1923 that administrative officers should receive training for their work, and that this training should include anthropology. But this could not be given with particular reference to New Guinea unless research were carried out. The Congress and then the Australian National Research Council called for such research and for money to make it possible. The response was good. We can now proceed to summarize the results of pre-1914 and post-1921 research.

There are several works of the survey type, which provide important anthropological information for parts of several Administrative Divisions (or Districts) in the Territory, and must be kept at hand for reference and background. Without such contributions we would be almost ignorant of what the local cultures were from, say, forty to seventy years ago. These works include:

J. Pfeil: *Studien und Beobachtungen aus der Südsee*, 1899, pp. 1-322. This gives a generalized picture of the individual's life from birth to death; of "Kanaka" psychology, religion and morals, and other aspects. The author's main interest is psychological. He travelled in the Bismarck Archipelago, the Admiralties and Buka, and also amongst the Jabim on the mainland.

Dr. M. Krieger: *Neu-Guinea*, 1899, devotes pp. 137-229 to the mainland of German New Guinea, principally to the tribes of Huon Gulf and Astrolabe Bay, amongst whom missions were working.

Dr. Rudolph Pöch: "Travels in German, British and Dutch New Guinea" *Geographical Journal*, Vol. 30, 1907, pp. 609-616; in a brief account of his work in 1904-6, refers to the Kai tribe on Sattelberg, the Monumbo, in the north-western end of the Madang District, and Laur, the central part of New Ireland.

G. Brown: *Melanesians and Polynesians*, 1910, which includes parts of New Britain and New Ireland in a comparative and general survey.

R. Neuhauss: *Deutsch Neu-Guinea*, Volume I, 1911, pp. 1-534; which covers his expedition in the Lower Markham Valley, in the Sattelberg region, and along the coast to Aitape and back to Finsch Harbour. He provides information according to a plan of inquiry for the peoples visited.

1. MOROBE DISTRICT

Commencing with the southern part of this District, we have Mr. Chinnery's report (*Anthropological Report*, No. 4, 1927) on his ethnological survey in 1927 from the Lower Waria to the Ono and Upper Waria, and across to the Biaru and the Bialolo. In this he gives notes and population figures for the Zia and Biawaria on the Lower Waria and some census figures for mountain groups. The language of the Upper Waria groups on the north and south of Mt. Chapman extends north to Mt. Lawson, and according to Mr. Chinnery, with few changes to the headwaters of the Bialolo. No research has been done in this inland region, although it was coming under control in the 1930's and mining was being done in the Upper Waria and Ono Valleys. However, the opportunity is still there, and should be considered. The population is not great. The 1937 figures for the Bubu, Ono, Upper Waria and Biaru, that is the southern inland corner of Morobe, adjacent to Papua, were 3,023. The present figure would be about 2,000 more. There are probably more people between the Biaru and the headwaters of the Bialolo, and the Biangai. An interesting reference to these people was made in the *Annual Report for the Territory of New Guinea* for 1924-25, pp. 98-108, by the Morobe District Officer.

An administrative officer at Lae who knows the district puts the Bubu at about 1,500, and regards them as the same people as the Kunimaipa across the Papuan border, where they number from 4,000 to 5,000. The Ono-speaking people, numbering no more than 1,500, extend from Susiwa and Gene along the Obo River up to Sini. Both the Bubu and the Ono have adopted European vegetables in their diet.

The Biaru and Biangai people are setting a health problem. Epidemics of pneumonia are reported to begin among them and to spread down the Waria, with some fatal results. This has its repercussions on employment, for the Waria was formerly the backbone of the native services. A medical and dietary survey is obviously needed, but sociological research should be associated with it. A teamwork project through the Waria, Biaru and Biangai is suggested.

Incidentally, Bia is the main Waria language and extends down to Biawaria on the Papuan border, though there are also two Bia-speaking villages (Eipa and Zinaba) a long way off, down the Lower Miai-mana.

In this same general interior region, but further north and west, are the so-called Kukukuku between the head of the Watut and Tiviri Rivers. A large population was reported on the Kapau. The people might be described as "nomadic" gardeners, shifting about and making new plots in the jungle. Contact of any enduring kind was not made until the 1930's, and in view of their wide range of territory, which crosses into Papua on the Upper Tiviri (the western branch of the Lakekamu), Tauri and Vailala, and of their inevitable "pacification" and culture-change, at least one sample of them should be studied as soon as possible.

Continuing north-west, there is a big group at the head of the Vailala, the Maralinen, who are probably still untouched, unless the Australian Petroleum Company has made contact with them. They can be reached from the head of the Tiviri.

In Lower Waria, the south-eastern coastal district of the Morobe Division, the Allied Geographical Section Terrain Survey shows 3,000 Southern Melanesians. These must be the Suenna, who include Kobo just south of the Waria mouth, and who, so I was informed by an administrative officer at Lae, came from Papua just before German control began. They extended northwards to the Miai-mana River, conquering or driving the local inhabitants away. Two Bia-speaking remnants on the latter river have been mentioned, while Sappa, Pose and Anna are also islands of an earlier language amidst a Suenna sea. This explains why when passing recently through a very large and well ordered garden near Dona village beyond Zaka Mission, our guide emphasized that the garden belonged to Sappa, not to Kobo (the Tsia-speaking or Suenna village) across the Waria. He felt definite pride, if not superiority, in the distinctness of his village and its language, even if it be but a remnant of a former greatness. Two or more generations of Lutheranism had not overcome this separateness.

References

E. W. P. Chinnery: "Natives of the Waria, Williams and Bialolo Watersheds". *Anthropological Report*, New Guinea, No. 4, 1927, pp. 1-64; (especially pp. 29-38).

E. W. P. Chinnery: "The Central Ranges of the Mandated Territory of New Guinea from Mt. Chapman to Mt. Hagen". *Geographical Journal*, Vol. LXXV, 1934, pp. 398-405.

Huon Gulf

In the coastal region, and moving away from Papua, the first place to be intensively studied is the village of Busama, a few miles north of Salamaua, consisting of 600 people. This is a culturally changed and Christianized native society which had undergone all the vicissitudes of war, Japanese domination and defeat, Australian military rule and later peace-time administration. As Dr. Hogbin began this research in September 1944, and has revisited Busama several times up to January 1950, a unique record of post-war re-adjustment is available. Several articles have appeared in *Oceania*, and a book on the village has gone to the publishers.[1] The population of Busama was enumerated in 1937 at 2,157.

For the Buang, a tribe of about 6,000 in the Snake River Valley, in the high country, thirty miles or so from Salamaua, we have Administrative officer L. G. Vial's account of their method of disposal of the dead, before it was changed about 1925 under missionary influence. The Buang work in the mines, but seldom for more than two years.

For Huon Gulf itself, in addition to the general survey material of Krieger and Neuhauss, there is an article by Dr. Hogbin on the revival of native trade around the Gulf after the recent war. An interesting aspect of this trade these days is the weekly arrival at Lae of canoes from Busama and the Markham with goods for sale at the Saturday market, which is run by the natives themselves. Europeans are among the buyers.

We have also an important series of articles on different tribes. S. Lehner, Lutheran missionary, has written a good deal on the Bukaua, between the Mange River and Lae, particularly with reference to their beliefs, cults and magic.

G. Bamler contributes a section (mainly on myths and legends) in R. Neuhauss, *Deutsch-Neu-Guinea*, Vol. III, 1911, pp. 489-566, on the Tami—a very small island community; H. Zahn provides a very useful account of the social organization of the Jabim on the point of the Huon Peninsula; Ch. Keysser, a long section on the Kai, which, unfortunately, does not examine the social structure, though it gives information under various headings, no doubt suggested by Neuhauss; and Stolz, a brief account of the Ono-speaking people, as he knew them in two villages with a population of 500 (Sialum and Kwam-Kwam), in the Cape King William district. Actually, Ono is the language between the Cromwell Range and Kalasa.

[1]This work was published in 1951 under the title *Transformation Scene.*—A. P. E., November 1952.

Further west, the packed community of little Sio Island was briefly studied in early 1934 by Mr. W. C. Groves; his results, which were significant and practical, were published in *Oceania*. His general conclusion was that in the case of Sio, a Christianized community, there should be as little interference as possible with the people in their everyday lives.

Thus, thanks almost solely to this missionary team, inspired by Neuhauss, we have good information, obtained at a time when the people concerned had been in contact with administration and missions for about thirty years. In 1937 there were about 17,000 in their districts. There does not seem to be any practical reason for intensive sociological research in this coastal region; but rather a general survey of the results of contact over the years. A mission anthropologist could give valuable help. The main task in all such situations is to gauge the degree of cohesion and self-direction of the society, and to see that the education, health and economic policies serve to ensure cohesion and self-direction. The Trust Territory of New Guinea and parts of Papua need several practical anthropologists, who, on the basis of past research and history, can sum up the present sociological and psychological condition of the communities.

The Markham Valley

The Huon Peninsula is bounded on the west by the Markham River. Three Lutheran missionaries—Pilhofer, Flierl and Keysser—set out from Sattelberg in 1912 and made an exploratory journey to the Markham and the Watub, inhabited by the Samuke, Ogau, Laewomba and Adjera (Atsera). Later on, the Lutherans reduced the Laewomba and Atsera languages to writing; these are spoken by about 2,000 and 5,000 people respectively, while the 3,000 Ameri, further up the Markham Valley, speak a dialect of the latter. K. E. Read has done basic sociological research amongst the missionized and "civilized" Ngarawapum group of villages in the Upper Markham between the Umi and Maniang branches. His research included a study into the effects of the war on the natives. In addition, we have a short account by Mr. Vial of an irrigation ceremony amongst the Wantoat population of 10,000, with special reference to Bumbum village.

Such a group presents an opportunity for research, but when so much is to be done it does not present an aspect of urgency.

References

H. I. Hogbin: "Local Government for New Guinea". *Oceania*, Vol. XVII, No. 1, 1946, pp. 38-67.

H. I. Hogbin: "Sex and Marriage in Busama, N. E. New Guinea". *Oceania*, Vol. XVII, No. 2, 1946, pp. 119-39. Vol. XVII, No. 3, 1947, pp. 225-48.

H. I. Hogbin: "Shame! A Study of Social Conformity in a New Guinea Village". *Oceania*, Vol. XVII, No. 4, 1947, pp. 273-89.

H. I. Hogbin: "Native Christianity in a New Guinea Village". *Oceania*, Vol. XVIII, No. 1, 1947, pp. 1-36.

H. I. Hogbin: "Pagan Religion in a New Guinea Village". *Oceania*, Vol. XVIII, No. 2, 1947, pp. 120-46.

H. I. Hogbin: "Government Chiefs in New Guinea", in *Social Structure*, Ed. by M. Fortes, 1949, pp. 189-206.

L. G. Vial: "Disposal of the Dead Among the Buang". *Oceania*, Vol. VII, No. 1, 1936, pp. 64-9.

H. I. Hogbin: "Native Trade Around the Huon Gulf, N.E. New Guinea". *Jnl. Polynesian Society*, Vol. 56, No. 3, Sept. 1947, pp. 242-55.

S. Lehner: "Bukaua". In R. Neuhauss, *Deutsch-Neu-Guinea*, Vol. III, 1911, pp. 397-485.

S. Lehner: "Geister und Seelenglaube der Bukaua". *Mitteilungen aus dem Museum für Völkerkunde*, 1930.

S. Lehner: "The Notion of Maja in the Jabem Language of N.E. New Guinea". *Jnl. Polynesian Society*, Vol. 41, No. 162, 1932, pp. 121-30.

S. Lehner: "The Balum Cult of the Bukaua of Huon Gulf, New Guinea". *Oceania*, Vol. V, No. 3, 1935, pp. 338-46.

S. Lehner: "Einige Gedanken zum Kapital 'frauenkang' bei den Eingeborenen in Huongulf nordösten Neu-guineas". *Mitteilungsblatt*, 1935, No. 5, pp. 14-24.

G. Bamier: "Tami". In R. Neuhauss, op. cit. pp. 489-566.

H. Zahn: "Die Jabim". In R. Neuhauss, op.cit. pp. 289-394.

Ch. Keysser: "Aus dem Leben der Kai-leute". In R. Neuhauss, op. cit. pp. 3-242.

Stolz: "Die Umgebung von Kap Konig Wilhelm". In R. Neuhauss, op. cit. pp. 245-86.

W. C. Groves: "The Natives of Sio Island, S.E. New Guinea". *Oceania*, Vol. V, No. 1, 1934. pp. 43-64.

Ch. Keysser: "Vom Sattelberg zum Markham". *Zeitschrift für Ethnologie*, Vol. XLIV, No. 12, pp. 558-84.

K. E. Read: "Social Organization in the Markham Valley, New Guinea". *Oceania*, Vol. XVII, No. 2, 1946, pp. 93-118.

K. E. Read: "Effects of the Pacific War in the Markham Valley". *Oceania*, Vol. XVIII, No. 2, 1947, pp. 95-117.

K. E. Read: "The Political System of the Ngarawapum". *Oceania*, Vol. XX, No. 3, pp. 185-223.

L. G. Vial: "The Dangagamun Ceremony of the Wantoat". *Oceania*, Vol. VII, No. 3, 1937, pp. 340-46.

L. G. Vial: "Some Statistical Aspects of Population in Morobe District, New Guinea". *Oceania*, Vol. VIII, No. 4, 1938, pp. 383-98.

There are, however, two other areas in the Morobe District where the need for research can be emphasized. The first is between the South Rawlinson and the head of the Markham, roughly the people of the south-east of the preceding Wantoat-Leron tribe. They are the Wain and Erap, enumerated as 8,728 in 1937. These people have worked on the goldfields, and have had very strong contacts, including the Japanese, who treated them harshly. No study has been recorded of their past or of their social structure and culture under change. In view of their experiences a preliminary inquiry might be made, to be followed, if thought of practical value, by intensive research.

The other area borders on the goldfields of Bulolo and Wau. It includes the Buang and Biangai groups, numbering in the 1939 Report 6,336 and 9,958 persons respectively. On the west are people who were not enumerated. No research has been done amongst these people, but in view of their position and their increased industrialization, it should be done.

Finally, the goldfields themselves present a call to research into (1) the life lived by the natives brought there; (2) the effect on their attitudes of the conditions under which they work and live; (3) the effect of their absences on family, social and village life; and (4) the way in which they settle back into village life. These types of problems are often discussed, but they have not been followed through in a systematic way. A woman worker could do important work in this regard amongst the women and children, in particular, who are left in the village. This whole project is specialized, and needs to be undertaken by persons fully cognizant of all its implications.

2. MADANG DISTRICT

The Coast

On the Madang District coast, a long settled region, little sociological research has been done, though several missionaries of the Society of the Divine Word have written on aspects of the cultures: A. Aufinger on houses and villages in Astrolabe Bay (Rai coast), and on weather magic on the Yabob (Yomba) Islands near Madang, the language of which is Graged (the *lingua franca* of the Lutheran Mission on the Rai coast); H. Hubers on music at Karkar Island; F. Vormann on village lay-out and housing, amongst the Monumbo, opposite ·Manam, and about their psychological characteristics, religion, morality, dances and initiation; J. Reiter on gardening and the division of labour between the sexes along the coast from Madang to Monumbo, and also west of the Sepik, from Wewak to Aitape; and G. Höltker on the Mambu religious cult in the Bogai district. Amounting only to 134 pages, and being mostly descriptive, these articles do not give an adequate picture of the Madang District coast.

Further material is available. The first European to live in the region was the Russian scientist N. N. Miklouho-Maclay. Landing on the shingle shore of Astrolabe Bay in 1871 he spent a little over twelve months there, and in 1876-77 another eighteen months. He made his headquarters near Bongu but got to know well other villages and peoples both along the coast and inland to the mountains and also on the islands. He named the area the Maclay Coast, since often known as the Rai Coast (Rai being considered a corruption of Maclay). His published anthropological observations on the Papuans of this coast give the earliest picture of them and of their way of life. When leaving the Maclay Coast in 1877, Maclay warned them against a type of European, differing from the scientist, who would inevitably come to their country, shooting, robbing and taking into captivity (black-birding). He advised them to avoid bloodshed and to retreat into the ranges. Between this and his brief third visit in March 1883, the inevitable had happened. Gold-seekers had landed and stayed for some time. The natives, after ensuring the safety of Maclay's house and equipment, retreated, deserting the villages of Bongu, Gorendu and Garagasi. They had learnt to suspect the white man. Contact of the wrong sort had begun to change the "nature" of the Papuan, as Maclay had already seen to be the case amongst the Papuan Koviai on the south-west of Netherlands New Guinea, near Triton Bay. From then on, both as a pioneer student of racial contact and as a humanitarian, Maclay worked for an international protectorate over the Maclay Coast; on behalf of the natives he protested against the contemplated German annexation. His guiding belief was that

"the era if not already here is close at hand when the subjects of civilized states of all parts of the world will treat a dark race as their fellow creatures according to the maxims of the law of the nations, and no longer as wild beasts to be trained to slavery or extirpated as noxious vermin." (in F. S. Greenop: *Who Travels Alone*, 1944).

Eventually, the Maclay Coast came with the rest of New Guinea under the Mandate and later the international trustee principle of administration, thus realizing something of Maclay's hope. Indeed, this Report and the South Pacific Commission itself are related to the practical application of that principle. Such, too, is the justification of this rather long reference to the work of a pioneer worker in the field of anthropology and culture-contact. Indeed, in view of the Cargo Cult in the area, his work is of special interest.

Many years later than Maclay, B. Hagen, in 1899, published his book on the natural history and people of Kaiser-Wilhelmsland, in which he paid special attention to the Bogadjim (or Tamo) culture in Maclay's area; six years later Dr. R. Pöch wrote a sketchy account of the dances of the Monumbo further west. Much later, Miss Wedgwood carried out field research in 1933 in the island of Manam, off Potsdam Harbour. Some of her results have appeared in *Oceania*. Finally, Mr. Peter Lawrence, in 1949-50, completed a study of the village of Sumau-Iwaiwa, about four days inland, midway between Madang and Bogadjim, in an area which has experienced much contact and missionary activity. It is also marked by a strong Cargo Cult movement.

Thus, some useful and good sociological material is available for the coastal region of the Madang District. The Rai coast, however, has been the scene of a Cargo Cult, and so too has the far north-western coast of the district, between Madang and the Ramu, where the attitude is one of hostility to whites—a hostility associated with wartime experience. The ship of the Cargo Cult has become an aeroplane for which aerodromes have been cleared. I suggest a sociological survey of the Rai coast in particular, and the immediate hinterland— the Finisterre Range region is almost unknown—as well as a survey of the Madang-Ramu area, to be followed by intensive research in a group with a cult. It should be remembered that no local language has been used on this coast—the Lutheran Mission introducing Graged from further north, and the Roman Catholic using pidgin. This may have some bearing on the rise of the cults in the region.

The population of the Rai Coast and hinterland was given in 1940 as 11,351.

Manam

Manam, which with Boisa Island, had 3,724 people in 1940, might well be revisited by Miss Wedgwood, to study the changes which time and events have wrought on these independent people and their way of life and thought. The language, a Melanesian one, has been well studied, and so would provide a means of entry into Manam thought by the returning anthropologist.

Karkar

Karkar is of special interest because the southern half is Melanesian (dialect Graged) and the northern, Papuan (Vaskia), 3,500 speaking the latter, and nearly 6,000 the former on Karkar and Bagabag. A useful study could be made here by a woman worker.

The Ramu

Practically no research has been done in the Ramu Valley or between it and the Finisterre Range on the south and the Adelbert Range on the north. The Mission of the Divine Word has penetrated some of the country and up the Ramu. The late Fr. Kirschbaum has given a few notes of a mountain tribe at Narongham and Sugarow ("Ein neuentdeckter Zwergstamm auf Neu-Guinea", *Anthropos*, Vol. 22, 1927, pp. 202-215).

Exploration and a preliminary anthropological survey are needed before deciding on any intensive work. There is, however, a pygmy region in the upper Ramu in the Atemble-Aiome district. Its extent is unknown. Only patient research will lead to an understanding of this shy people and contribute to their progress.

References

Albert Aufinger: "Siedlungsform und Hauserbau an der Rai-Küste Neuguineas". *Anthropos*, Vol. 35-36, 1940-41, pp. 109-30.

Albert Aufinger: "Welterzauber auf den Yabob-Inseln von Neuguinea". *Anthropos*, Vol. 34, 1939, pp. 277-91.

Hubert Hubers: "Kleine musikethnologische Beiträge von der Insel Karkar in Neuguinea". *Anthropos*, Vol. 37-40, 1942-45, pp. 122-26.

Franz Vormann: "Dorf-und Hausanlage bei den Monumbo, Deutsch Neuguinea". *Anthropos*, Vol. 4, 1909, pp. 660-8.

Franz Vormann: "Zur Psychologie, Religion, Soziologie & Geschichte der Monumbo-Papua (Deutsch Neuguinea)". *Anthropos*, Vol. 5, 1910, pp. 407-18.

Franz Vormann: "Tänze und Tanzfestlichkeiten den Monumbo-Papua (Deutsch Neuguinea)". *Anthropos*, Vol. 6, 1911, pp. 411-27.

Franz Vormann: "Die Initiationsfeiern der Jünglinge und Mädchen bei den Monumbo-Papua, Deutsch Neuguinea". *Anthropos*, Vols. 10-11, 1915-16, pp. 159-79.

J. Reiter: "Der Ackerbau in Neuguinea und auf den angrenzenden Inseln". *Anthropos*, Vol. 3, 1908, pp. 234-38.

Georg Höltker: "Die Mambu-Bewegung in Neuguinea. Ein Beitrag zum Prophetentum in Melanesien". *Annali Lateranensi*, Vol. 5, 1941, pp. 181-219.

N. N. Miklouho-Maclay: *Ethnologische Bemerkungen über der Papuas von der Maclay Küste*. (Pamphlet), 1875.

N. N. Miklouho-Maclay: *Anthropologische Bemerkungen über der Papuas von der Maclay Küste*. (Pamphlet), 1873.

N. N. Miklouho-Maclay: Sobranie Sochinenii v pyati tomakh; five volumes being published, Moscow.

B. Hagen: *Unter den Papua's: Beobachtungen und Studien über Land und Leute, Thier-und Pflanzenwelt in Kaiser Wilhelmsland*, 1899, pp. 1-327.

F. S. Greenop: *Who Travels Alone*, 1944 The best book on Maclay and his work.

Dr. Rudolph Pöch: "Beobachtungen über Sprache, Gesänge und Tänze der Monumbo: Zulässlich phonographischer Aufnahmen in Deutsch-Neu-Guinea". *Mitteilungen der Anthropologischen Gesellschaft in Wien*, Vol. 35, 1905, pp. 230-37.

C. H. Wedgwood: "Report on Research in Manam Island, Mandated Territory of New Guinea". *Oceania*, Vol. 4, No. 4, 1934, pp. 373-404.

C. H. Wedgwood: "Sickness and its Treatment in Manam Island, New Guinea". *Oceania*, Vol. 5, No. 1, 1934, pp. 64-80; No. 3, 1935, pp. 280-308.

C. H. Wedgwood: "The Life of Children in Manam". *Oceania*, Vol. 9, No. 1, 1938, pp. 1-30.

C. H. Wedgwood: "Girls' Puberty Rites in Manam Island, New Guinea". *Oceania*, Vol. 4, No. 2, 1933, pp. 132-56.

C. H. Wedgwood: "Women in Manam". *Oceania*, Vol. 7, No. 4, 1937, pp. 407-29; Vol. 8, No. 2, 1937, pp. 170-93.

Fr. Kirschbaum: "Ein neuentdeckter Zwergstamm auf Neu-Guinea". *Anthropos*, Vol. 22, 1927, pp. 202-15.

Alois Kaspruch: "Der grobe 'prähistorische' Steinmörsen in Atemble am mittleren Ramu River in Neuguinea". *Anthropos*, Vol. 35-36, 1940-41, pp. 647-54.

T. G. Aitchison: "Peace Ceremony as Performed by the Natives of the Ramu Headwaters, Central New Guinea". *Oceania*, Vol. 6, No. 4, 1936, pp. 478-81.

Moyne, Lord, and Haddon: "The Pygmies of the Aiome Mountains, Mandated Territory of New Guinea". *J.R.A.I.*, Vol. 66, 1936, pp. 269-90.

3. THE CENTRAL HIGHLANDS DISTRICT

The first information about the peoples of this interesting region came from the exploring parties, usually administration patrols, in the 1930's. Some of the officers had done a short course in anthropology at the University of Sydney, and were therefore aware of the importance of the observations of natives and native life which they could make. Accounts of these patrols appeared in the Annual Reports on the Territory to the League of Nations. For example:

1938-39: R. I. Skinner, for the Mairifutika Valley, pp. 21-22.

J. L. Taylor, the Hagen-Sepik Patrol of 1938-39, pp. 139-49.

J. L. Taylor and John Black were the patrol officers in this latter Patrol.

Missionaries pushed into the district as soon as it was opened up, and began the study of the languages in the neighbourhood of their selected stations. This work has been summarized by Dr. Capell, *Oceania*, Vol. XIX. Later they were able to contribute to our anthropological knowledge of the Highlands, and were the pioneers in this field, with the exception of Dr. R. F. Fortune; he worked on Kainantu possibly amongst the Taiora-speaking people at the Kamamentina headwaters in the period when the area was far from controlled, and research was difficult.

Eastern Central Highlands

No research has been done, apart from this, in the eastern subdivisions of the Highlands. There are several large linguistic groups: the Agarabi (6,000), and the Taiora (about 12,000) in the Kainantu sub-district; the Forei, numbering about 20,000, in the same sub-district but in the region extending towards, and two days' walk over, the Papuan border, directly above the Purari River; the people are the Gurangga. Population fails altogether between the Western Purari and the Mukukuku of the headwaters of the Vailala. East of the Taiora are 6,000 or more Gadsup, and indeed, in the midst of the former, there are five small villages speaking Gadsup. Beyond the Taiora there are also two small tribes, as yet unknown. According to a recent patrol conducted by Mr. G. Toogood, Assistant District Officer, the Taiora linguistic group proper ends at Suwaira, but dialects of it extend down the Lamari on its eastern side as far as Pintata. This was determined by the ease or difficulty with which Taiora interpreters could make progress. Across the Lamari from the junction of the Azana and in the Azana Valley, the language is entirely different and appears to be allied to Forei. This, however, must be checked. Hote, spoken south-south-east of Kainantu, is a dialect of Taiora. On the west of the Kainantu aerodrome and between the headwaters of the Ramu and the Aiamantina, are about 7,000 Komanu, making a total for the whole Kainantu sub-division of about 50,000.

Obviously, there is great and pressing opportunity for research in this area, amongst almost unknown peoples. In July 1950 I saw, at Kainantu station, natives from new country who had just come in with the recent patrol to learn more of the ways of the white man and his administration. All the peoples of the sub-division are village dwellers, the villages which I saw being in oblong formation with a cleared space in the midst.

There is a note of urgency to be struck here, for changes in the native economy may well be fairly rapid in the nearer parts. A Government Agricultural Station has been established at Aiyura, and tea successfully grown. Coffee has been grown by several villages both here and in the sub-district, and bought by the Administration. Also 7,000 pounds of English potatoes a month have been purchased from the natives and sent to Lae and Madang. The natives take a great interest in road-making in this and in the Bena sub-division, being quite expert at grading and draining them. Moreover, they use the roads. A group of Finschhafen natives are gold-mining with success on the Wanton River near Kainantu. Thus money is coming to be appreciated, and to be spent at the several trade stores. Settlement of affronts in court is taking the place of killings. Finally, the missions are active, though more recently in Kainantu than in Bena.

Here then, is an opportunity and need to study a people settling down under a contact situation—the effects of changes in the economic sphere, of road-making and peaceful travel, of courts instead of combat—the effects of these and other factors on the social structure and on the psychological and physical well-being need to be known, if administration is to proceed towards its goal. It is a task for a social anthropologist with linguistic ability. Either the Taiora or the Gadsup group would seem to be the best to work in the first instance.

Passing into the Bena sub-district we see villages consisting of single lines of low circular houses. Around Bena-Bena and towards Garoka are the Hofaguk, numbering over 7,000, although Pastor Helbig who had been at Asaloka, a few miles north-west of Garoka, since about 1932, puts the true Hofaguk at 3,000. The language of the Garoka district is Gafuguk, which he considers could be called Gama. Up to 12,000 people understand Gama, in spite of dialectal differences. Pastor Helbig is now working on a dictionary, and I urged on him the duty of completing a grammar and texts in Gafuguk. The Sianei, southern neighbours of the latter, number five or six thousand, or even more, and the Kofera (Ofera) on the west, something over one thousand. There are a number of other small tribes in the same general district, like the Gaviyufa (500) and the Yabiyufa (1,000) on the south bank of the Gafugu River; and the Gurumbu (Gururumpa) (1,000) to the north-west, bordering on the Kuman in the Chimbu region. The Lambau on the south-east are not known.

Here is another opportunity for studying peoples, still living almost, and in many cases completely, in their traditional manner; but beginning to change.

One interesting change in the eastern end of the Bena sub-division was reported by a patrol in February 1950, of the Kamamentina and Gafutina Valleys: the former hamlet system is giving place to village units of from 70 to 300 persons. The houses are typical of the sub-division, being round or obloid, domed, and built of split planks and kunai.

In this particular area, with a population of 6,263, there is a population problem. In the majority of villages there are ten adult females to nine adult males, polygyny absorbing the surplus women. In the ten to sixteen age group, however, the position is very different, males being to females as four to two; at least this is common in the area. Moreover, the average family group has decreased over the past generation. This is a problem for a social anthropologist and a medical expert. Probably, then, for the Bena sub-district this project should receive priority.

The need for this is further emphasized by the fact that the Bena-Bena people are going out to work at an increasing rate; and research is required to keep a check on the effect of this development, including the effect of the introduction of European currency. This should go hand-in-hand with medical observation and care, and with a close watch on population statistics.

On the other hand, the Gafuguk in the Garoka neighbourhood, who have worked locally for the District Officer, have changed very little. There are a number of related tribes, and a thick population. Here, then, is an opportunity to study a highland society and culture before it has begun to change under the impact of spreading non-native interests, and demands and opportunities. The worker, however, must be prepared to master, and work in, the native language, and to spend at least two substantial periods in the field.[1]

Western Central Highlands

Passing west, we come to the peoples speaking quite distinct languages from the preceding, and living in homestead-garden fashion instead of in hamlets or villages. It is a region where both linguistic and anthropological research have made some progress. The main features of the languages have been summarized by Dr. Capell in *Oceania*, March, 1949.

The Chimbu Sub-district

Passing into the Chimbu sub-district, we have the large language group, generally known as the Kuman. Chimbu is the name of the river, while Kamanugu, by which the language is sometimes called, is the name of a small tribe in the larger group. The language has some peculiarities which make it difficult. It is tonal, though it is doubtful whether the tones are semantic. Discussion with Pastor Bergmann who, with a good linguistic background, has worked at Kundiava for about sixteen years, and my own brief observations, suggest that short vowels are usually of high tone and long vowels

[1]In 1950–1951 Dr. K. E. Read, on a Fellowship from the Australian National University, worked along these lines in the neighbourhood of Garoka; and in November, 1951, Mr. and Mrs. R. M. Berndt, under the auspices of the University of Sydney, began a similar project in the Kainantu area. In September, 1951, Dr. R. F. Fortune of Cambridge, England, returned to the Kamamentina headwaters, where he began research in 1935.—A.P.E., November 1952.

of low tone. Further, the difference between long and short vowels does affect meaning. The tone would help to differentiate this meaning. Thus *ga:ga* is boy, but *gaga* is stretcher; *du:* is straight or clever, *du* is stupid or deaf, and *wa:m* is son, but *wam* is fat. In each case, the long vowel is a high tone and the short one a low tone. The deep gutturals, the lateral velar fricatives and the latter assimilated to the next sound, all cause trouble. Still, it can be mastered; and it is worth while. Eighteen thousand have been counted in the tribe west of the Chimbu; on the east side, the estimate is 6,000.

The Janggamugl (7-8,000) speak a slightly varied dialect but understand Kuman and from Kundiava to one and a half hours beyond Kerowahgi, at least 6,000, including the 4,000 Gende (or Bundi) at Mingende, understand or speak it, making a total of about 40,000. In addition the Sinasina, numbering at least 10,000, south of Chimbu, understand Kuman without difficulty. So do their associates: a southern, and as yet un-numbered, people called by the Kerowahgi, the Boumai (meaning southwards, or seaward, or forest country); the Dom (about 10,000) who are very closely related to the Sinasina, and include the Yani (in the middle of the Marel River Valley); and the big group estimated at up to 15,000, called Tjuavre (the name of the Government Post). Thus there are possibly another 40,000 to whom Kuman can become a regional language.

Moreover, all over this area the culture is much the same. This applies to festivals and dances, gardening methods, the homestead system, and the ceremonial use of archaeological objects to which power of fertility is attributed. Villages are only built for meetings, such as ceremonies connected with pigs. Some difference, however, appears among the Gende, who show cultural affinity with the Ramu.

Two of the Chimbu tribes have been studied anthropologically by missionaries. First, John Nilles has published articles on the Kuman of the Bismarck Mountains, a people living at a height of from seven to over eight thousand feet. His thesis for the Diploma of Anthropology (Sydney) on the "Social Organization and Culture of the Kuman" will be printed in *Oceania*.[1] Second, H. Aufenanger has recorded much of the culture of the Gende, and this, edited by Fr. G. Höltker, has been published as a book. It deals well with material culture, ritual, magic and myths, but the social organization needs more examination.

---

[1]This appeared in the September 1950 issue under the title, *The Kuman of the Chimbu Region, Central Highlands, New Guinea.*—A. P. E., November 1952.

Fr. Aufenanger has also written on the Gende system of counting. Fr. A. Schaeffer has given us an interesting, though brief, account of a Chimbu man's life-history—from Koruguru, and of an initiation ceremony. He is concerned with the Chiambugla and neighbouring peoples on the southern slope of the Bismarck Ranges.

This district presents opportunities for research. At Chimbu the contact has not been intense, but it has in a period of fifteen years had some effect, though not on the social structure. The unexpressed reactions to administration are important, and the study of them in such an area would be helpful. I have asked Fr. Nilles to continue his studies of the Kuman, paying special attention to the effect of contact on various aspects of the culture.

There is also a population problem looming. Pastor Bergmann informed me that some men in Chimbu—and a greater proportion in Hagen—were unmarried, because there were not enough women. The count in four districts around four rest-houses showed that two female to three male children were being born and that the same proportion was true of the adults. This is very serious in a region so thickly populated and from which much progress is hoped. The facts should be investigated, and if correct, the causes sought.[1]

North-west of the Kuman, two days' walking from Chimbu, are the Kuno, who occupy a sparsely populated area on the southern slopes of the Range. They are gardeners, but their culture is different from that of the Kuman. There are no mission stations in their country, though mission teachers have been amongst them, and there are some police stations. Here, then, is an almost "untouched" tribe, waiting to be studied.

Hagen Area

The best known name of the whole region is Mt. Hagen, and the people in the vicinity have been more subjected to contact influences than those elsewhere in the Highlands. The tribes form a language group, somewhat different from the Chimbu people; several of the Wahgi Valley tribes and also the Kuno belong linguistically to the Hagen group. There is a growing literature on the Hagen people proper. The Rev. W. Ross (Society of the Divine Word), who was

[1] Work of this nature is being done in the Marind-anim district of Netherlands New Guinea as a project of the South Pacific Commission. Dr. H. J. Bijlmer and Dr. S. Kooijman are in charge of the investigations.— A.P.E., November 1952.

in the district before the war, published some notes in 1936 on the Mogei, a Hagen clan in the vicinity of the Government Station. F. E. Williams, in the following year, published further notes, based mainly on information supplied by Fr. Ross; and this applies also to A. L. Gitlow's *Economics of the Mt. Hagen Tribes*, 1947, a useful study, although it is obvious that the author himself did not know the culture. The main work on the area, however, has been *Die Mbowamb: Die Kultur der Hagenberg-Stämme im Ostlichen Zentral-Neuguinea* (3 vols.) 1943-8, by G. V. Vicedom, a Lutheran missionary who had been four years in the district, and H. Tischner of the Hamburg Museum. This is a thorough study of what happens in the life of the people, including culture-change, and of their spiritual beliefs and outlook. It provides an excellent basis for further work. The people studied by Mr. Vicedom centred on the Lutheran Mission at Ogelberg, five miles from Fr. Ross' station, and speak a related dialect.

The Hagen dialects, Medlpa and Tjimbagik (Tembaga), are spoken by over 40,000. The total for the sub-district is about 100,000, including Mindj or the middle Wahgi Valley. The Tjika tribe is said to be the largest in the sub-district. The population density has to be seen to be grasped. Thus at a feast at Ulga (Orlgu) about 10,000 people were present. They killed 762 pigs. A patrol in 1949 counted over 7,000 people in the Nebilyer Valley (south of Hagen, but still in the Trust Territory), and 3,000 in a small group on the southern bank of the Wahgi. And a recent patrol of one week only in the Nembi Valley in Papua, north-east of Lake Kutubu, was amongst what an experienced officer considered to be about 12,000 people. To look around the valleys and hills, however, one would not suspect the presence of anything like these numbers, so well are the homesteads set in the gardens. This is also true of Wabag sub-district.

The people of the south bank of the Jimmi River are of Hagen type, but the language changes northward at this river. Fr. Ross of Hagen doubts whether the Kuno can understand Medlpa. Kuno is the name given by the Hagen people to the "bush people" beyond Nondugl, just as they call those near Chimbu, Kune, and those towards the junction of the two arms of the Jimmi, Korbin. The eastern boundary of the Medlpa is the Tuman River, across which the middle Wahgi dialects are not as yet studied. On the west, Romba (Tomba) village on Mt. Hagen itself is the limit; beyond is the Tjaga (or Tsaga) called Enga by the Hagen people. On the south of the Medlpa are the Gawil

(Kauil) in Papua, which is only about fifteen miles from Hagen. Dr. Capell considers these languages closely related. This means that the anthropologist with a good grounding in Medlpa could accommodate himself elsewhere in the sub-district.

As there is little doubt that Medlpa should, or at least could, become the regional native language for this great group of people—great in numbers and in bearing—extending into Papua in the Nembi and the Waga Valleys, it is most unfortunate that the two missions working in the language hear and spell it differently, and do not collaborate in the matter. The errors in one case are obvious, nor does any consideration of practicability justify the omission of significant sounds or the inconsistent use of symbols.

In this and in any other similar cases, the administration concerned, through its education department, might be well advised to call a conference with an expert linguist as chairman and final arbiter. He would, of course, test sounds with the native speakers, and then decide on the most suitable symbols to be used, bearing in mind costs and printing problems, and that the aim is a literature in the vernacular. His decision should be accepted. Otherwise, there must be confusion and the arbitrary breakdown of a language.

A most important practical problem of research in this sub-district and also in Wabag (and indeed in Chimbu too), is that of land ownership and use. This demands not only a knowledge of the social structure, but also of the history of the local groups, this history being usually of comparatively recent events. Wars have caused local groups to migrate and to settle in other parts, generally with the consent of those owning the land whither they fled. Some kinship, exchange or ceremonial link was at the back of this arrangement. Now, however, that Pax Australiana is being forced on the region, these refugees come to the district officers asking for the land from which they had been driven by conquerors to be restored to them. This is no simple matter for judgement or adjudication.

Another problem arises when, as at Nondugl Experimental Sheep Farm, the native owners, to gain "profit", willingly sold the land to the Trust, for they themselves were not using it. Seven hundred others, former "wartime" refugees and "tenants", had, with the consent of their owner-friends, been depending on it and had come to regard its usufruct as theirs. They are now landless—a very serious condition for homestead gardeners. The employment of 130 men for varying periods and from various places, on the Sheep Farm, does not solve this "landless" problem. Obviously, the present use to which the original land of the 700 or their parents and grandparents is being put must be discovered, and some allotment made. Once again, however, it is not as simple as it may sound.

Likewise, the resumption of 1,000 acres, even for such a good purpose as a hospital, may (as has occurred) affect the land-owning rights and the livelihood of about 7,000 people. In the same way, resumption during the war, of a not very big area of level land at Wabag for a small landing strip, but necessarily garden ground, was partly responsible for non-co-operation on the part of the natives concerned.

These incidents are only mentioned to illustrate the need for research into land ownership and use, and its many ramifications.[1] I suggest that this be done first in the Nondugl district, and then near Hagen; and that this be correlated with similar inquiry to be carried out as part of an intensive anthropological project at Wabag. At the same time, in each district, the important exchange and compensation ceremonies should be studied, for they are probably related to the land question, as well as to war, "trade" and religion.

In addition, the plan to put a Government Post in the Nembi or Waga area and to admit missionary activity means that, if possible, an anthropologist should be ready to go straight in, study the language, social structure and culture, and so provide the understanding which both administration and mission require. Moreover, these people (in part the Waga-furari spoken of by Hides), tucked away in their valley, have been enjoying, right up to this moment, a self-contained and self-directed life, with only such outside contacts as brought them what they desired. Such a phenomenon is fascinating, and should be studied for the purpose of throwing light on man and his communal relationships. Two recent patrols have gained the friendship of these people—even if it is as yet only passive friendship.

Wabag Sub-district and Beyond

Passing Romba on Mt. Hagen and also a point twenty-two miles north of Hagen Station, we come to the large population, reckoned as up to 120,000, speaking Tsaga and related dialects, westward to beyond Porgera (Porgubieri). This cultural and linguistic area extends

[1]e.g., K. E. Read: "Land in the Central Highlands". *South Pacific*, Vol. 6, No. 7, 1952, pp. 440-9.

south to the Tari in Papua, amongst the Tarifuroro spoken of by Hides, culture-originators in his opinion—the big-wig people. They are referred to as the Hoiyevia. A patrol along the Lai, Minyamp, Wagime, Tari and Tobak Rivers counted 25,284 people. The Sau and Maramuni, north of Wabag, are in the same general group, though a patrol officer has reported nomads, the Heja, from the latter. They do not possess pigs. It is to be hoped, however, that the Heja will be studied soon, and an attempt made to help them adjust themselves in the change from nomadism to settled life. The problem may be similar to that which faces the Australian Aborigines.

There has been little contact in the Wabag sub-district. J. Hides, *Papuan Wonderland*, patrolled through the Papuan side of it in 1935, and J. L. Taylor gives a few interesting notes in the Annual Report for the Mandated Territory, 1938-39, p. 145.

During an all too brief visit in July, 1950, I began a study of the kinship system, and of the important exchange system called the Te. Patrol Officer Brightwell in the course of census work has made a preliminary analysis of the group structure of the people around Wabag. As in the Hagen and Wahgi Valleys, the Tsaga have no villages, but build their houses (separate for husband and wives) in their gardens. They are mound gardeners, and use a type of *in situ* compost system. The population is dense. I saw 2,500 at one "Fair" two miles from the station, and next day 2,000 at another one mile nearer, and few were the same people.[1]

I regard Wabag as a first priority for research amongst what is, almost everywhere in the sub-district, an untouched culture and people. At present they are non-co-operative with the Administration, but they respect it and are not really hostile. Killing still goes on with axe and arrow, but gradually the court is dealing with these happenings and indeed, forestalling them. Mission work, begun near Wabag in 1946, has not advanced far, but two missionaries near Wabag are gaining some knowledge of the language and culture. A couple of miners have had no effect on the people and their way of life.

This is an ideal area for the five year intensive type of project referred to in the section on principles of research. Moreover, anthropological help is needed by the Administration; amongst the problems are the many implications for law, employment and economics, of

[1]A preliminary report on the social organization and the Te will appear in *Oceania*, 1953. See also, G. A. M. Bus: "The Te Festival or Gift Exchange in Enga". *Anthropos*, Vol. 46, 1951, pp. 813-24.

the great Te delayed-exchange system, which comes to a head about every three and a half years; it needs to be studied throughout its whole cycle, from the time articles leave Wabag to go east, and the return goods (pigs, gold-lip shell and other objects) have slowly reached their destination and are ceremonially handed over. Other problems are land ownership and the effect of past wars; compensation for killings; and the psychological attitude of the people to the Administration. This is a field of research of practical value, and of inestimable interest to science.

Much further west is Telafomin and the sub-district bearing its name, included in the Central Highlands District, but administered, because of transport convenience, from Wewak. The sub-district extends along the headwaters of the Sepik and the Fly to the Netherlands border. The Karius-Champion expedition from Papua in 1927-28 passed through it and J. L. Taylor's patrol of 1938 went west as far as Telafomin. A Government Post has now been established there and patrols are being carried out. The country is rugged and poor. The population is sparse, numbering just over 4,000. A start has been made with the language.

Both linguistic and anthropological research is required in this area which in both aspects probably crosses both the Trust Territory of New Guinea-Papuan border and also the Netherlands border. This coincides with what has already been said with regard to the north-west corner of Papua.

References

A. Capell: "Distribution of Languages in the Central Highlands, New Guinea". *Oceania*, Vol. 19, Nos. 2, 3, 4, 1948-9, pp. 104-30, 234-54, 349-78.

E. W. P. Chinnery: "Mountain Tribes of the Mandated Territory of New Guinea from Mt. Chapman to Mt. Hagen". *Man*, 1934, No. 140, 8 pages.

M. J. Leahy, "Stone Age People of the Mount Hagen Area". *Man*, 1935, No. 202, pp. 185-6.

R. F. Fortune: "The Rules of Relationship Behaviour in one variety of Primitive Warfare". *Man*, 1947, pp. 108-110.

J. Nilles: "Die Siedlungsform bei den östlichen Waugla u. Kurugu im Wagital Neuguineas". *Anthropos*, Vol. 33, 1938, pp. 664-70.

J. Nilles: "Häuserbau und Häuserformen bei den östlichen Waugla u. Kurugu im Wagital Neuguineas". *Anthropos*, Vol. 33, 1938, pp. 963-8.

J. Nilles: "Digging-sticks, spades, hoes, axes and adzes of the Kuman people in the Bismarck Mountains of East-Central New Guinea". *Anthropos*, Vols. 37-40, 1942-45, pp. 205-12. (Articles edited by G. Höltker).

J. Nilles: "Natives of the Bismarck Mountains, New Guinea". *Oceania*, Vol. 14, No. 2, 1943, pp. 104-24; Vol. 15, No. 1, 1944, pp. 1-19.

J. Nilles: "The Kuman of the Chimbu Region, Central Highlands, New Guinea". (Thesis for the Diploma in Anthropology, University of Sydney). *Oceania*, Vol. 21, No. 2, pp. 25-65.

J. Nilles: "Mädchen-Reiferfeier bei den östlichen Waugla im Bismarckgebirge Neu-guineas". *Anthropos*, Vol. 34, 1939, pp. 402–6.

J. Nilles: "The Initiation of Boys among the Waugla in New Guinea". *Internationales Archiv f. Ethnographie*, Vol. 38, 1940, pp. 93–8.

H. Aufenanger: Etwas über Zahl u. Zählen bei den Gende im Bismarckgebirge Neu-guineas". *Anthropos*, Vol. 33, 1938, pp. 273–7.

H. Aufenanger & G. Höltker: *Die Gende in Zentral Neuguinea:* Vom Leben und Denken eines Papuastämmes in Bismarckgebirge. 1940, pp. 1–201.

Alphons Schaeffer: " 'Kavagl', der Mann mit der Zaunpfahlkeule".—Ein Beitrag zur Individuen-forschung. *Anthropos*, Vol. 33, 1938, pp. 107–113.

Alphons Schaeffer: "Zur Initiation im Wagi-Tal". *Anthropos*, Vol. 33, 1938, pp. 401–23.

Alphons Schaeffer: "Ein Frauenbegrabnis bei den Korugu im Wahgi Tal". *Ethnos*, Vol. 7, 1942, pp. 25–43.

W. Ross: "Ethnological Notes on Mt. Hagen Tribes (Mandated Territory of New Guinea)". With special references to the Tribe called Mogei. *Anthropos*, Vol. 31, 1936, pp. 341–63.

F. E. Williams: "The Natives of Mount Hagen, Papua: Further Notes". 1937, pp. 90–6.

L. Meiser: "Beitrag zum Thema: Gerichtswesen bei den Mogä im Neuguinea". *Anthropos*, Vol. 33, 1938, pp. 663–4.

A. L. Gitlow: "Economics of the Mount Hagen Tribes, New Guinea". 1947, pp. 1–110.

G. V. Vicedom & H. Tischner: *Die Mbowamb: Die Kultur der Hagenberg-Stämme im Ostlichen Zentral-Neuguinea.* (3 vols. 1943–8).

J. J. Murphy: "Stone Workers of New Guinea, Past and Present". *Oceania*, Vol. 9, No. 1, 1938, pp. 37–41.

L. G. Vial: "Stone Axes of Mount Hagen, New Guinea". *Oceania*, Vol. 11, No. 2, 1940, pp. 158–64.

W. Kienzle & S. Campbell: "Notes on the Natives of the Fly and Sepik River Head-waters, New Guinea". *Oceania*, Vol. 8, No. 4, 1938, pp. 463–81.

J. Hides: *Papuan Wonderland*, 1936, pp. 77–106.

I. E. Champion: *Across New Guinea from the Fly to the Sepik*, 1932, pp. 1–267.

4. THE SEPIK DISTRICT

Passing into the Sepik Administrative District from the Central Highlands, and moving down the river, we have J. W. M. Whiting's and S. W. Reed's anthropological field-work results for the Kwoma in the hills, near Ambunti, on the Upper Sepik, together with the earlier observations of Behrmann and Roesicke. The Kwoma number something less than 1,000. Another river village, Yesam, twenty miles upstream from Ambunti, has a language like Kwoma.

For the middle Sepik there is Gregory Bateson's work on the Iatmul (including his *Naven*) near Palimbai, and not far to the south, Dr. M. Mead's research amongst the Tchambuli on Ribom Lake, a people numbering about 500, and further east, amongst the Mundugumor, a community on the Yuat River about 1,000 in number in 1932, which had been under full Government control for about three years. Each of these two communities speaks a language different from Iatmul.

The great Sepik River Valley is not thickly populated, consisting so much of swamp or kunai grass country. The population from Wogamush to the mouth is estimated at 36,000. The Iatmul language (Angoram, Palimbai and Burui) links up with the Maprik (Abelam) language which extends from Wos(h)era to villages four hours' walking north of Maprik, for the most part a thickly populated area, blessed with rich soil. As a coastal outlier, so to speak, the Boikin language at Boikin and Wewak is closely related. Indeed, a missionary used the Boikin grammar amongst the Iatmul and found it satisfactory. The culture is marked significantly by the very tall men's ceremonial houses with their painted beak-shaped fronts. Dr. Phyllis Kaberry did field research in 1939-40 in the village of Kalabu near Maprik, and has published articles on the basic social and political organization, and more is to follow. In spite of some missionary activity, now being intensified; in spite of about 150 Abelams, or Tshwosh (Tsosh, bush Kanaka) as the Iatmul call them, going away each month to work for varying periods; and in spite of trade stores and administration, the Abelam culture has not changed much. It is obvious that apart from the men in their twenties the people still prefer the old ways. More-over, as I saw, though returned men and hospital employees may have feigned lack of interest in the old customs, they took part in cere-monies, their only concession to modernity being the use of a lava-lava round their loins. It is doubtful whether iconoclastic methods by one or other of the missions will do more than drive some practices, sacred objects and ceremonies "underground". Indeed, some actions by the missionaries are apt to be interpreted as magical. One result of contact is the sticking of pictures from magazines on the lower part of the fronts of the ceremonial houses. Initiation rites are still held in all their former detail, as I saw in July 1950, and the custom of burying the dead under a special structure right against the village prevails— a slight modification of burying the corpse within the house. The house is in either case deserted, and possibly some property destroyed.

Next to the Abelam are the Arapesh, who speak But. They were studied in 1931-32 by Dr. Margaret Mead and Dr. R. Fortune. They form an arc on the north, west and south-west of the Abelam, ex-tending south from But and Suein to Yamil and Ulapu, two hours' walking east of Maprik, but further south on that side. They "swing" down the western side by Sipari, and on to the Sepik Plain.

Dr. Mead's research in the region embracing the Arapesh, Tcham-buli and Mundugumor, with their wide economic and social relations, gives her an embracing knowledge of the Wewak, Ambunti, Keram triangle. I suggest, therefore, that Dr. Mead be asked to return to the region for a six months' (or longer) survey to study its present economic and social life and to report on any changes which have occurred. This should be done, whether or not Dr. P. Kaberry returns to the Abelam and Mr. Bateson to the Iatmul.

Dr. Fortune has written on Arapesh warfare, as well as on the language, and missionary A. Gerstner on yam cultivation and feasts in the But district.

The population of the Maprik sub-district is 44,000, consisting chiefly of Abelam and Arapesh and some Iatmul.

For the south of the Sepik we have only Dr. R. Thurnwald's work on the Banaro, high up the Karen River, and his note on the Tjimundo.

In the south-west, pygmies have been reported from the Schrader Range. They are possibly connected with those of Mt. Aiome, but almost nothing is known of them.

References

J. W. M. Whiting & S. W. Reed: "Kwoma Culture". Oceania, Vol. 9, No. 2, 1938, pp. 170-217.
J. W. M. Whiting: Becoming a Kwoma: Teaching and Learning in a New Guinea Tribe, 1941, pp. 1-227.
A. Roesicke: "Mitteilungen über Ethnographische Ergebnisse der Kaiserin Augusta-Flüss-Expedition". Zeitschrift für Ethnologie, Vol. 46, 1914, pp. 507-22.
W. Behrmann and A. Roesicke: Im Stromgebiet des Sepik, 1922.
G. Bateson: "Social Structure of the Iatmul People of the Sepik River". Oceania, Vol. 2, No. 3, 1932, pp. 245-92; No. 4, pp. 401-54.
G. Bateson: Naven: A Survey of the Problems suggested by a Composite Picture of a Culture of a New Guinea Tribe from Three Points of View, 1936, pp. 1-286, with 28 plates.
M. Mead: Sex and Temperament in Three Primitive Societies, 1935, pp. 1-335.
R. F. Fortune: "A Note of Some Forms of Kinship Structure". Oceania, Vol. 4, No. 1, 1933, pp. 1-10.
R. Thurnwald: Die Gemeinde der Banaro, 1921.
R. Thurnwald: "Banaro Society, Social Organization and Kinship System of a Tribe in the Interior of New Guinea". Memoirs American Anthropological Association, Vol. 3, No. 4, 1916.
R. Thurnwald: "Some Traits of Society in Melanesia". Proceedings of the Fifth Pacific Science Congress. Vol. IV, 1933, pp. 2805-14.
A. J. Marshall: The Men and Birds of Paradise, 1938; pp. 1-299.
R. Thurnwald: "Adventures of a Tribe in New Guinea (The Tjimundo)" in Essays Presented to C. G. Seligman, 1934, pp. 345-60.
P. M. Kaberry: "The Abelam Tribe, Sepik District, New Guinea". Oceania, Vol. 11, No. 3, 1941, pp. 233-59; No. 4, 1941, pp. 345-68.
P. M. Kaberry: "Law and Political Organization in the Abelam Tribe". Oceania, Vol. 12, No. 1, 1941, pp. 79-96; No. 3, 1942, pp. 209-26; No. 4, 1942, pp. 331-64.
M. Mead: "The Marsali Cult Among the Arapesh". Oceania, Vol. 4, No. 1, 1933, pp. 37-54.
M. Mead: "The Mountain Arapesh. I. An Importing Culture". Anthropological Papers, American Museum of Natural History, XXXVI, Pt. III, pp. 145-349. (Published as one volume).

M. Mead: "The Mountain Arapesh. II. Supernaturalism". *Anthropological Papers*, American Museum of Natural History, XXXVII, Pt. III, pp. 319-452. (Printed separately).

M. Mead: "The Mountain Arapesh. III. Socio-Economic Life. IV. Diary of Events in Alitoa". *Anthropological Papers*, American Museum of Natural History, Vol. 40, Pt. 3, 1947, pp. 163-419. (Printed separately).

R. F. Fortune: "Arapesh Warfare". *American Anthropologist*, Vol. 41, 1939, pp. 22-41.

Andreas Gerstner: "Der Yams-Anbau im But-Bezirk Neuguineas". *Anthropos*, Vol. 34, 1939, pp. 246-66.

P. Kirschbaum: "Ein neuendeckter Zwergstamm auf Neu-Guinea (Schrader Range)." *Anthropos*, Vol. 22, 1927, pp. 202-15.

Sepik District Coast

For the Sepik District coastal region as a whole, apart from the Arapesh, we have to rely so far only on contributions from missionaries of the Society of the Divine Word, although G. Friederici, on the basis of his expedition to the German Territory in 1908, and of published material, has provided a good introductory study of several coastal peoples: at Ser (Sir), Malol and Aitape. He was concerned with describing material culture and observable customs, rather than with sociology.

For the district at the mouth of the Sepik, J. Schmidt describes and discusses the life of the people from Karau to Murik and Kaup. J. Gehberger, missionary at Turubu, records myths from Samap (a Melanesian-speaking village). P. W. Schmidt describes and discusses initiation on the Karesau Islands, west of Wewak. F. Vormann describes the daily life of the Valman people, east of Aitape; while several contributions have been made for the peoples from Matapau to Aitape: H. Meyer, a detailed and functional examination of the Parak Cult and of the Wunekau (Sun-god) Cult; and Jacob Blaes on childbirth customs, missionary influence on these, and on children's song-games.

The only other information, with one exception, is for the Vanimo coast, for which K. H. Thomas, formerly an administrative officer, gives a survey of the culture. The exception is the research carried out by Dr. Hogbin in 1934 on the island of Wogeo, at the western end of the Schouten group, and some distance off Wewak. A long series of articles on the Wogeo was published during 1935-46. The Island had been regularly recruited for thirty years and traders visited it. A mission teacher had just been established. Dr. Hogbin suggested in his first report, 1935, that "the culture would in all probability have modified itself within the next few years." A return visit by Dr.

Hogbin, if only for a short period, should define the present condition and trend of this island society. It numbered then about 900. Likewise, Miss Wedgwood should be invited to return to Manam, and one of these two workers might pay some attention to the island of Koil, near Wogeo.

As for the coast itself, there does not seem to be any urgent practical need for research, though, if the Parak Cult be still in existence, a woman worker could study the relation of that Cult to women and, in addition, make a thorough study of the social structure and life of the community.

More important is a sociological survey of the coast from the Sepik mouth to Wewak, where the Kanaka Cargo Cult flourished. As this is on a great trading route, Cargo Cult influence can easily spread.

There are other interesting places for research, such as Irimu, a day in from Wewak, a district characterized by bark paintings; and the first tributary of the Sepik, where a Feather Cult and the use of profile figures stand out.

The population in 1940: Vanimo coast, 1,231; Aitape coastal villages, 5,666; Islands off Aitape, 893; Wewak coast (south to Mindam), 3,629; Schouten Islands, 2,057. That is, about 13,000 along the coast, apart from those at the mouth of the Sepik. The Vanimo hinterland, 2,823, and the Aitape and Wewak hinterlands, the large figure of 102,243, with the Sepik River, another 35,809 (that is, up to Wogamush).

These figures, when compared with the amount of research done, show a big task which lies ahead. There is still a good deal of the country not well controlled, including the Bewani Mountains in the west, and much of the hinterland of Aitape.

In the latter is the Dreikirkir district with a population of over 19,000, in which no research has been carried out. Planes go in and out frequently to the Administrative Post there, and work could be done, though I suggest a preliminary survey be made to determine whether the culture is significantly different from the Arapesh or Abelam. The language is different. An anthropological and linguistic expedition to the Vanimo hinterland working amongst the Bimbi, Kilmeri and other tribes, and also along the Netherlands border would help to fill in the gap. Perhaps Dutch and Australian or other scientists could combine in this, but it must be admitted that the population is very sparse.

References

G. Friederici: *Wissenschaftliche Ergebnisse einer amtlichen Forschungsreise nach dem Bismarck-Archipel im Jahre 1908*, Vol. II, "Beiträge zur Völker und Sprachenkunde von Deutsch Neu-Guinea", 1912, pp. 1-324, and illustrations.

Joseph Schmidt: "Die Ethnographie der Nor-Papua (Murik-Kaup-Karau) bei Dall-mannhafen, Neuguinea". *Anthropos*, Vols. 18-19, 1923-4, pp. 700-32; Vol. 21, 1926, pp. 38-71.

Joseph Schmidt: "Neue Beiträge zur Ethnographie der Nor-Papua (Neuguinea)". *Anthropos*, Vol. 28, 1933, pp. 321-54, 663-82.

J. Gehberger: "Aus dem Mythenschatz der Samap an der Nordost-Küste Neuguineas". *Anthropos*, Vol. 45, 1950, pp. 295-342; 733-78.

W. Schmidt: "Die geheime Jünglingsweihe der Karesau-Insulaner (Deutsch-Neu-guinea)". Nach den Mitteilungen des Karesau-Insulaners Bouifaz-Tarnatai Pritak". *Anthropos*, Vol. 2, 1907, pp. 1029-56.

Fritz Vormann: "Das tägliche Leben der Papua (unter besonderer Berücksichtigung des Valman-Stammes auf Deutsch-Neuguinea)". *Anthropos*, Vols. 12-13, 1917-18, pp. 891-909.

Heinrich Meyer: "Das Parakwesen in Glauben und Kult bei den Eingeborenen an der Nordostküste Neuguineas".(Introduction by Georg Höltker). *Annali Lateranensi*, Vol. 7, 1943, pp. 95-181.

Heinrich Meyer: "Wunekau, oder Sonnen verehrung in Neuguinea". *Anthropos*, Vol. 27, 1932, pp. 423-55, 819-54; Vol. 28, 1933, pp. 27-53.

Jacob Blaes: "Brauchtum bei der Gebert eines Kindes auf den Inseln am Berlinhafen Nordost-Neuguinea". *Anthropos*, Vols. 41-44, 1946-49, pp. 853-74.

Jacob Blaes: "Die Kinder-Singspiele auf der Insel Ali, Nordost-Neuguinea". (Intro-duction by Georg Höltker). *Anthropos*, Vols. 41-44, 1946-49, pp. 119-60.

K. H. Thomas: "Notes on the Natives of the Vanimo Coast, New Guinea". *Oceania*, Vol. 12, No. 2, 1941, pp. 163-87.

H. I. Hogbin: "Adoption in Wogeo, New Guinea". *Journal of the Polynesian Society*, Vol. 44, No. 4, 1935, pp. 208-215; Vol. 45, No. 1, 1936, pp. 17-38.

H. I. Hogbin: "Native Culture of Wogeo". *Oceania*, Vol. 5, No. 3, 1935, pp. 308-38.

H. I. Hogbin: "Trading Expeditions in Northern New Guinea". *Oceania*, Vol. 5, No. 4, 1935, pp. 375-408.

H. I. Hogbin: "Tillage and Collection: A New Guinea Economy". *Oceania*, Vol. 9, No. 2, 1938, pp. 127-52; No. 3, 1938, pp. 286-326.

H. I. Hogbin: "Social Reaction to Crime: Law and Morals in the Schouten Islands, New Guinea". *J.R.A.I.*, Vol. 68, 1938, pp. 223-63.

H. I. Hogbin: "Native Land Tenure in New Guinea". *Oceania*, Vol. 10, No. 2, 1939, pp. 113-66.

H. I. Hogbin: "The Father Chooses his Heir: A Family Dispute over Succession in Wogeo, New Guinea". *Oceania*, Vol. 11, No. 1, 1940, pp. 1-40.

H. I. Hogbin: "A New Guinea Infancy". *Oceania*, Vol. 13, No. 4, 1943, pp. 285-310.

H. I. Hogbin: "Marriage in Wogeo, New Guinea". *Oceania*, Vol. 15, No. 4, 1945, pp. 324-53.

H. I. Hogbin: "A New Guinea Childhood". *Oceania*, Vol. 16, No. 4, 1946, pp. 275-97.

H. I. Hogbin: "Puberty to Marriage: A Study of the Sexual Life of the Natives of Wogeo, New Guinea". *Oceania*, Vol. 16, No. 3, 1946, pp. 185-209.

M. F. Leask: "Tools of a Canoe-Building Industry from Cape Wom, Northern New Guinea". *Oceania*, Vol. 17, No. 4, 1947, pp. 300-10. Map, p. 301.

5. MANUS DISTRICT

This district includes a number of small islands in addition to the Admiralty group. The populations of the former are small.

In 1940 they were:

Wuvulu	248	Hermit	25
Aua	225	Anchorite	1
Ninigo	263		

They have received some attention from observers, Parkinson (16 pages), Dempwolff, who speculated on the voluntary dying-out of the inhabitants, and G. L. F. Pitt-Rivers who visited Aua in 1921. This island is estimated to have had a population of probably 1,500 in 1903, but nearly 700 were drowned in 1904 when trying to get away from the island after a clash with two white settlers. By 1921 the number was down to about 300. Epidemics and a disturbance of the birth-rates and death-rates bear on the problem. Possibly the unventilated houses are also connected with it, as tuberculosis is prevalent. Wuvulu (Maty) and the Hermit group present the same problem of depopulation. A medical survey, rather than anthropological research, seems indicated. Incidentally, Ninigo, which decreased from 400 in 1921 to 263 in 1940, is not too small to have had a Cargo Cult.

The population in the Admiralty Islands, however, has held its own, being 12,688 in 1940. Under Government control since 1912, its people had made a good adjustment to the new economic factors (indentured labour, pay and trade), and to the loss of certain prohibited customs. They are an advanced and "prosperous" people who are driving ahead into this modern world. During the War they suffered under the Japanese, and their way of life was interfered with by the huge allied occupation. They are an independent people, and on the resumption of civil administration expressed their intention of not signing on for labour, though in 1946 I saw a small group offering to work for the District Officer, and to find replacements when they returned home. I realized too that the Manus people had much reconstruction of villages and remaking of gardens to do, and also many mourning obligations to fulfil on behalf of those who were killed in the War. In spite of this, by 1948, 75 were working for the Administration, 88 were indentured and 293 were working for private employers without indentures, a total of 456. In 1949, the number was down to 360. In 1939, however, 696 Manus were indentured in the Admiralties, and the same number elsewhere. There is need on Manus of an objective sociological inquiry into the present conditions, attitudes and aspirations of the Manus, some indication of which is given by their strong desire to learn English—as distinct from pidgin, which is the *lingua franca*, and the only speech known to some of them.

After all, the men of the Allied Forces spoke English. This research should, of course, cover all the groups—there are 23 languages and their cultures.

I have stressed the above facts lest it be felt, as I have seen stated in the press, that the unwillingness of the Manus to offer in the number required for essential works is an indication that they had been spoilt. It should be pointed out that they paid dearly for our War, and had "to put their own house in order."

It is important that the Manus "drive" be guided wisely, and yet not thwarted, or else they may become resentful and at least non-co-operative. They are a worth-while people.

Fortunately, we have some good earlier research results on which to base further study. In addition to the earlier material of Parkinson and J. Meier, and A. Bühler's brief notes, we have the all-round anthropological research carried out by Dr. Fortune and Dr. Mead in 1928-9. The latter discussed the effect of contact in an appendix to her *Growing Up in New Guinea*. If Dr. Mead comes to survey the Sepik area with which she was familiar, I hope she will also be able to make this survey of the Manus.[1]

References

R. Parkinson: *Dreissig Jahre in der Südsee*, pp. 209-25.
Dr. Dempwolff: "Über aussterbende Völker (Die Eingeborenen der 'Westlichen Inseln' in Deutsch Neuguinea)". *Zeitschrift für Ethnologie*, Vol. 36, 1904, pp. 384-415.
G. L. F. Pitt-Rivers: "Aua Islands: Ethnographical and Sociological Features of a South Sea Pagan Society". *J.R.A.I.*, Vol. 55, 1925, pp. 425-38.
G. L. F. Pitt-Rivers: *The Clash of Culture*, 1927, pp. 272-5.
R. Parkinson: *Dreissig Jahre in der Südsee*, pp. 174-208.
Josef Meier: "Mythen und Sagen der Admiralitäts-Insulaner". *Anthropos*, Vol. II, 1907, pp. 646-67, 933-41; Vol. III, 1908, pp. 193-206, 651-71; Vol. IV, 1909, pp. 354-74.
A. Bühler: "Versuch einer Bevölkerungs—und Kultur-analyse auf den Admiralitäts-inseln". *Zeitschrift für Ethnologie*, Vol. 67, 1935, pp. 1-32.
R. F. Fortune: "Manus Religion". *Oceania*, Vol. 2, No. 1, 1931, pp. 74-109.
R. F. Fortune: *Manus Religion*, 1935, pp. 1-391.
M. Mead: *Growing Up in New Guinea: A Comparative Study of Primitive Education*, 1930, pp. 1-372.
M. Mead: "Kinship in the Admiralty Islands". *Anthropological Papers*, American Museum of Natural History, Vol. XXXIV, Pt. II, pp. 183-358.

6. THE NEW IRELAND DISTRICT

The Smaller Islands

Passing east from the Admiralties to the first group in the New Ireland District—Saint Matthias, Parkinson (*Südsee*, pp. 159-73) gives

[1]The latter is planned for 1953.—A. P. E., November, 1952.

a few notes, including a short history of contact, but Mr. Chinnery has done the only anthropological research on the group, concentrating on Emirau where he spent two months amongst its 424 people, and nine days on St. Matthias with its 1,619 persons. The population was then (1925) increasing. The 1940 figures suggest a slight decrease.

A check might well be made of the population, present social structure and manner of life. This is work that Mr. E. W. P. Chinnery, a master of "sociological census", might be asked to do.

Lavongai (New Hanover) off the western end of New Ireland, has never been studied, though Parkinson refers to it. Mr. Chinnery has some knowledge of it. It is a region marked by strict avoidance of rules and by a suicide sanction. Leprosy is rampant, and this has kept field-workers at bay. However, there need be no risk. The population in 1940 was 2,330 males and 2,858 females, a total of 5,188.

Along the north-east of New Ireland are several groups of islands, in two of which anthropological research has been carried out. Mr. William C. Groves was in Tabar, mainly at Tatau village, in 1933. His results have appeared in a series of articles, very definitely of practical as well as scientific value. Special attention should be paid to the contact position.

On Tanga Mr. F. L. S. Bell made a thorough functional study on Boieng in the Tanga group in 1933, and has published a very fine series of articles, and much more is to come. The population of these two groups in 1940 was 1,952 and 1,778 respectively.

No research has been done on Lihir, 3,394, Feni, 913, or Nuguria, 69, except what Mr. Chinnery has been able to do in the course of visits on administrative duty.

New Ireland Mainland

For New Ireland Parkinson gives a short general description. Two research projects were conducted on the northern coast—one by Mr. Groves in 1933 at Fisoa, in which he paid special attention to culture-contact and to the part education should play in the progress of the people. The village contained about 200 persons and the linguistic group of which it forms a part numbers 1,484. The second project was conducted in 1929 by Miss H. Powdermaker at Lesu, one of a group of five villages speaking one language. In addition to

Life in Lesu, she made an important study of the population problem in Lesu and also in the Kavieng District, New Ireland. Lesu itself, with a population of 222, was decreasing because of a rising death-rate, while the birth-rate was, at best, static. Kavieng figures available for 1928-29 show that the decrease was general. ("Vital statistics in New Ireland", *Human Biology*, 3, 1931, pp. 351-375.)

An excellent census, with notes on the social structure and vital statistics, was collected in 1929 by Mr. Chinnery amongst 68 village divisions on the "East Coast of New Ireland" from Kavieng to Karu. The problem of depopulation was being faced, for this had been shown by Dr. Hoffman in 1912 to be serious. Such work, to be of use, must be followed up from time to time. It is good to know, therefore, that after nearly three years of representation, Mr. Chinnery has been enabled to return and re-survey the position. His report that the decrease has not been checked has a bright aspect: the people are ready to take a grip on themselves and co-operate with administrative efforts to turn the tide.

Incidentally, Mr. Chinnery's field-sociological approach to the taking of a census, by living in the villages so as to get the "feel" of the people and to ascertain their attitudes, is essential.

Missionaries of the Sacred Heart Order have made several contributions on aspects of the culture of New Ireland: G. Peekel, for the Namatanai district, on kinship and marriage, religious beliefs and sorcery (*Religion und Zauberei auf dem mittleren Neu-Mecklenburg*, 1910), religious dances, the "Malanggan" at Tombara, and the Moon Cult; Fr. Abel on children's games; and Fr. K. Neuhauss on beliefs in a Supreme Being amongst the Pala, Namatanai district. In addition A. Krämer wrote on the Malanggan at Tombara (1925).

For the eastern part of southern New Ireland, Emil Stephan (a surgeon who visited the area in 1904) and F. Graebner (ethnologist), have given us a useful picture of native life, of "material and spiritual culture", along the coast from Cape St. George west and north to Umuddu; and Dr. O. Schlaginhaufen, a few notes on the Butam.

There is little to recommend in the way of anthropological research in this Island of a long history of contact and small population— 19,417 in 1940. "Welfare" work and economic development, with guidance from Mr. Groves on the basis of his earlier field-work, and advice from Mr. Chinnery, an experienced District Officer, should ensure the people's advance.

96   SOCIAL ANTHROPOLOGY IN MELANESIA

References

R. Parkinson: *Dreissig Jahre in der Südsee*, pp. 159-73.
E. W. P. Chinnery: "Notes on the Natives of Emirau and St. Matthias". *Anthropological Report* No. 2, 1925, pp. 1-238.
E. L. Piesse: "Decline of Population in the Territory of New Guinea". *Proceedings of Pan Pacific Science Congress* (Aust.) 1923, Vol. 1, pp. 241-2.
W. C. Groves: "Fishing Rites at Tabar". *Oceania*, Vol. 4, No. 4, 1934, pp. 432-58.
W. C. Groves: "Tabar To-day: A Study of a Melanesian Community in Contact with Alien Non-Primitive Cultural Influences". *Oceania*, Vol. 5, No. 2, 1934, pp. 224-41; No. 3, 1935, pp. 346-61; Vol. 6, No. 2, 1935, pp. 147-58.
W. C. Groves: "Tabar To-day". Part II. *Oceania*, Vol. 6, No. 2, 1935, pp. 147-58.
W. C. Groves: "Secret Beliefs and Practices in New Ireland". *Oceania*, Vol. 7, No. 2, 1936, pp. 220-46.
W. C. Groves: "Settlement of Disputes in Tabar". *Oceania*, Vol. 7, No. 4, 1937, pp. 501-20.
F. L. S. Bell: "Report on Field Work in Tanga". *Oceania*, Vol. 4, No. 3, 1934, pp. 290-310.
F. L. S. Bell: "Warfare among the Tanga". *Oceania*, Vol. 5, No. 3, 1935, pp. 253-80.
F. L. S. Bell: "The Avoidance Situation in Tanga". *Oceania*, Vol. 6, Nos 2 and 3, 1935-6, pp. 175-99, 306-25.
F. L. S. Bell: "Death in Tanga". *Oceania*, Vol. 7, No. 3, 1937, pp. 316-40.
F. L. S. Bell: "Courtship and Marriage among the Tanga". *Oceania*, Vol. 8, No. 4, 1938, pp. 403-19.
F. L. S. Bell: "Sokapana: A Melanesian Secret Society". *J.R.A.I.*, Vol. 45, 1935, pp. 311-41.
F. L. S. Bell: "The Play Life of the Tanga". *Mankind*, Vol. 2, No. 3, pp. 56-61; Vol. 2, No. 4, pp. 83-6.
F. L. S. Bell: "The Narrative in Tanga". *Mankind*, Vol. 3, No. 2, pp. 57-67; No. 3, pp. 80-8; No. 11, pp. 330-4; No. 12, pp. 361-6. Vol. 4, No. 1, pp. 24-31.
F. L. S. Bell: "The Place of Food in the Social Life of the Tanga". *Oceania*, Vol. 17, No. 2, 1946, pp. 139-72; No. 4, 1947, pp. 310-27. Vol. 18, No. 1, 1947, pp. 36-60; No. 3, 1948, pp. 233-48. Vol. 19, No. 1, 1948, pp. 51-75.
F. L. S. Bell: "The Industrial Arts in Tanga". *Oceania*, Vol. 19, No. 3, 1949, pp. 206-34. Vol. 19, No. 4, 1949, pp. 320-49.

References: New Ireland Mainland

R. Parkinson: *Dreissig Jahre in der Südsee*, pp. 130-49.
W. C. Groves: "Report on Field Work in New Ireland". *Oceania*, Vol. 3, No. 3, 1933, pp. 325-62.
W. C. Groves: "Divazukmit—A New Ireland Ceremony". *Oceania*, Vol. 3, No. 3, 1933, pp. 297-312.
H. Powdermaker: "Report on Research in New Ireland". *Oceania*, Vol. 1, No. 3, pp. 355-65.
H. Powdermaker: "Mortuary Rites in New Ireland (Bismarck Archipelago)" *Oceania*, Vol. 2, No. 1, 1931, pp. 26-44.
H. Powdermaker: "Vital Statistics in New Ireland". *Human Biology*, 1931, pp. 351-75.
H. Powdermaker: *Life in Lesu*, 1933, pp. 1-349.
E. W. P. Chinnery: "Studies of the Native Population of the East Coast of New Ireland". *Anthropological Report*, No. 6, 1929, pp. 1-50.
G. Peekel: "Die Verwandtschaftsnamen des mittleren Neu-Mecklenburg". *Anthropos*, Vol. 3, 1908, pp. 456-81.
G. Peekel: *Religion und Zauberei auf dem mittleren Neu-Mecklenburg*, 1910, pp. 1-135.
G. Peekel: "Religiose Tänze auf Neu-Ireland (Neu-Mecklenburg)". *Anthropos*, Vol. 26, 1931, pp. 513-32.
G. Peekel: "Die Ahnenbilder von Nord-Neu-Mecklenburg. Eine kritische und positive Studie". *Anthropos*, Vol. 21, 1926, pp. 806-24; Vol. 22, 1927, pp. 16-44.
G. Peekel: "Uli und Ulifeier oder vom Mondkultus auf Neu-Mecklenburg". *Archiv. für Ethnologie*, Vol. 23, 1932, pp. 41-75.

Abel: "Knabenspiele auf Neu-Mecklenburg, Südsee". *Anthropos*, Vol. II, 1907, pp. 219-29, 708-14. *N.B.* Continuation of article started in Vol. I.

K. Neuhauss: *Beobachtungen und Studien Der Missionare vom hlst. Herzen Jesu in der Südsee.* Band I. "Das Höchste Wesen etc. amongst the Pala, Mid-New Ireland", 1934, pp. 1-105.

A. Krämer: *Die Malanggane von Tombara*, 1925.

A. Krämer: "Tomboresisches, Altes und Neues". *Anthropos*, Vol. 22, 1927, pp. 803-10.

E. Stephan & F. Graebner: *Neu-Mecklenburg: Die Küste von Umuddu bis Kap St. Georg*, 1907, pp. 1-242.

Dr. Otto Schlaginhaufen: "Die Rand-Butam des östlichen Süd-Neu-Mecklenburg". *Zeitschrift für Ethnologie*, Vol. 40, 1908, pp. 803-9.

Dr. Otto Schlaginhaufen: "Uber Siedelungs-Verhältnisse in Süd-Neu-Mecklenburg". *Zeitschrift für Ethnologie*, Vol. 42, 1910, pp. 822-9.

J. A. Grump (Rev.): "Trephining in the South Seas". *J.A.I.*, Vol. 31, 1901, pp. 167-73.

7. THE NEW BRITAIN DISTRICT

Gazelle Peninsula

The coastal districts of the large island of New Britain became well-known during the period of the German Administration. Travellers and missionaries gradually recorded information about the native peoples, especially about those in the Gazelle Peninsula. Parkinson published a book in 1887, *Im Bismarck-Archipel*, in which he covered the history and problems of contact, and also gave a general description of the customs, rites and beliefs of the people in the Peninsula. He refers to the same region, including the Baining groups (Taulil, Butam and Sulka), and also the the western part of the Island in his *Südsee*. Emil Stephan, surgeon, visited the Peninsula and eastern New Ireland, and published a useful work in 1907 on the art of the two regions. Finally, Graf von Pfeil gave, in 1897, a good account of the Duk Duk and native "mystery", and of the upheaval caused by European contact.

Two Methodist missionaries began writing on the peoples of the Peninsula in the 1890's, after being several years there. These were George Brown who began on Duke of York Island in 1875, and Benjamin Danks who settled on the mainland in 1878. Their contributions were mainly papers to meetings of the Australian Association for the Advancement of Science, except for Brown's later *Melanesians and Polynesians*, which dealt in part with New Britain. *In Wild New Britain*, 1933, edited from B. Danks' Diary is interesting from the point of view of culture-contact. A much later contribution by a Methodist missionary was an article on the Kuanua in *Oceania*, 1940, by J.W. Trevitt, which in spite of its brevity reflects the value of even a short course in anthropology, such as the missionaries of the Methodist Missionary Society have been taking at the University of Sydney during the past seventeen years.

The preceding writings have been mainly about the people around Blanche Bay, who, within a radius of twenty miles of Rabaul, were estimated at about 30,000 in 1940. Roman Catholic Mission work was begun in the same district early this century, and before long began contributing to *Anthropos*. Fr. J. Meier wrote on the religious and magical and idea beliefs, and the Iniet Society of the Blanche Bay natives; C. Laufer on the social behaviour; J. Winthuis on their marriage customs and character; Fr. O. Meyer on the Sun Festival, mythology, and fishing amongst the people on Vuatom, and J. Meier added a short account of the Sun Festival. G. Bögerhausen wrote on the string-games and their songs at Matupit. On the north-west coast of the Peninsula, a brief general account was given by F. Hees in 1915-16.

In 1906 the Rev. A. Kleintitschen published *Die Küstenbewohner der Gazellehalbinsel*, about the Livuan-speaking tribe, on the east of the Peninsula, an indispensable record of the culture of nearly fifty years ago. He devotes a chapter to two slave-tribes—the Baining and Taulil.

The Baining

Quite a literature has grown up about the Baining peoples, though in a small way, but they have not yet been well studied. The population of the Bainings was given in 1940 as 6,296 and for the Sulka-Timoip, 2,839. In addition to Parkinson and Kleintitschen, Thurnwald visited them twice, Fr. Bley recorded myths from the north-west Baining, and Fr. C. Laufer, in an article on the concept of a High-God amongst three Baining groups, gives a very useful summary of previous research on this people and also refers to the effects of the Japanese invasion. The Snake Dance fascinates, and three articles on it have appeared in *Oceania*. A good anthropological survey of the Baining peoples and their culture would be welcomed.

No research has been done on the north coast, that is, east and west of Talasea. Here, however, there is a definite anthropological task, especially inland east of Talasea. A people, called the Mokolkol, rush on to the coast from time to time causing trouble, but nothing is known of them. A link with them needs to be established by the Administration, and an anthropological study would provide the necessary understanding.

On the south coast one research project has been carried out, but unfortunately, only a small part of the results has been written up. This was at Moewehaven, where Mr. J. A. Todd worked in 1933 and 1935. Mr. Chinnery, in 1925, gathered some information for this coast, especially at Gasmata, Moewehaven and Arawi.

There is still much to be learned about the interior and mountainous region of this Island. An anthropological survey is suggested to cross the island from west of Moewehaven, following the Olimpit River, up to the Whiteman Range, and then working down to the north coast. This would need to be a properly organized patrol, and should be given ample time to make an adequate preliminary survey of the people and their prospects of development.

At the west end of New Britain is Dampier Strait and a number of islands. Umboi (or Rooke) Island and the Siassi group are the chief, with a population in 1940 of 4,781. Umboi is a mixture of Melanesian and some Papuan elements. With Tami near the New Guinea mainland, they form a trading group. A companion study of Umboi and Siassi is required, such as Mr. Groves did for Sio, which is also in the trade "ring".

Trade routes need studying not only out of economic interest, but because ideas also pass along them. In this case, Cargo Cult ideas could so pass, for Sio is linked in trade with the Rai Coast, where the Cargo Cult has been present.

References

R. Parkinson: *Im Bismarck-Archipel: Erlebnisse und Beobachtungen auf der Insel Neupommern*, 1887, pp. 1-154.

R. Parkinson: *Dreissig Jahre in der Südsee*, pp. 47-129.

Emil Stephan: *Südseekunst: Beiträge zur Kunst des Bismarck-Archipels und zur Urgeschichte der Kunst überhaupt*, 1907, pp. 1-145. (Refers to eastern New Ireland as well as to Gazelle Peninsula).

Graf v. Pfeil: "Duk Duk and other Customs as forms of expressions of the Melanesians' Intellectual Life". *J.A.I. of G.B. and I.*, Vol. 27, 1897-8, pp. 181-91.

B. Danks (Rev.): "New Britain and Its People". *Australian Association for the Advancement of Science*, Hobart, 1892, Vol. IV, pp. 614-20.

B. Danks (Rev.): "Some Notes on Savage Life in New Britain". *Australian Association for the Advancement of Science*, Brisbane, 1909, Vol. XII, pp. 451-7.

G. Brown (Rev.): "Life History of a Savage". *Australian Association for the Advancement of Science*, Sydney, 1898, Vol. VII, pp. 778-90.

G. Brown (Rev.): "Some New Britain Customs". *Australian Association for the Advancement of Science*, Melbourne, 1901, Vol. VIII, pp. 307-12.

100   SOCIAL ANTHROPOLOGY IN MELANESIA

G. Brown (Rev.): "Notes of a Recent Journey to New Guinea and New Britain". *Australian Association for the Advancement of Science*, Sydney, 1898, Vol. VII, pp. 790-7.

B. Danks: *In Wild New Britain*, 1933, pp. 1-293. Edited by W. Deane.

J. W. Trevitt: "Notes on the Social Organization of N.E. Gazelle Peninsula, New Britain". *Oceania*, Vol. 10, No. 3, 1940, pp. 350-60.

Josef Meier: "Primitive Völker und 'Paradies'-Zustan. Mit besonderer Berucksichtigung der früheren Verhältnisse beim Oststamm der Gazelle-Halbinsel im Bismarck-Archipel (Neupommern)". *Anthropos*, Vol. 2, 1907, pp. 374-86.

Josef Meier: "A Kaja, oder Der Schlangenaberglaube bei den Eingeborenen der Blanchebucht (Neupommern)—Ein Beitrag zur Geschichte der Religion den primitiver Völker". *Anthropos*, Vol. 3, 1908, pp. 1005-29.

Josef Meier: "Der Glaube an den Inal und den Tutana Vurakit bei den Eingeborenen im Küstengebiet der Blanchebucht". *Anthropos*, Vol. 5, 1910, pp. 95-112.

Josef Meier: "Die Zauberei bei den Küstenbewohnern der Gazelle-Halbinsel, Neupommern, Südsee". *Anthropos*, Vol. 8, 1913, pp. 1-11, 285-305, 688-713.

Carl Laufer: "Einige Anstandsregeln der Qunantuna auf Neubritannien". *Anthropos*, Vols. 41-44, 1946-9, pp. 349-56.

J. P. Winthuis: "Kultur und Karakterskizzen aus der Gazellehalbinsel, Neupommern, Südsee". *Anthropos*, Vol. 7, 1912, pp. 875-92; Vol. 9, 1914, pp. 914-47.

J. P. Winthuis: "Heiratsgebräuche bei den Gunantuna auf Neupommern". *Anthropos*, Vol. 22, 1927, pp. 765-92.

Josef Meier: "Steinbilder des Iniet-Geheimbundes bei den Eingeborenen des nordlichen Teiles der Gazelle-Halbinsel, Neupommern, Südsee". *Anthropos*, Vol. 6, 1911, pp. 837-67.

Josef Meier: "Der Totemismus in Bismarck-Archipel. Melanesien, Südsee". *Anthropos*, Vols. 14-15, 1919-20, pp. 532-42.

Otto Meyer: "Ein Sonnenfest bei den Eingeborenen von Vuatom. Neupommern, Südsee". *Anthropos*, Vol. 3, 1908, pp. 700-1.

Otto Meyer: "Mythen und Erzählungen von der Inseln Vuatom, Bismarck-Archipel, Südsee". *Anthropos*, Vol. 5, 1910, pp. 711-33.

Otto Meyer: "Fischerei bei den Uferleuten des nördlichen Teiles der Gazellehalbinsel und speziell auf der Inseln Vuatom, Neupommern, Südsee". *Anthropos*, Vol. 8, 1913, pp. 82-109, 325-41, 1069-1103.

Josef Meier: "Die Feier der Sonnenwende auf der Insel Vuatom, Bismarck-Archipel, Südsee". *Anthropos*, Vol. 7, 1912, pp. 706-721.

Georg. Bögerhausen: "Fadenspiele in Matupit, Neupommern". *Anthropos*, Vols. 10-11, 1915-16, pp. 908-12.

Friedr. Hees: "Ein Beitrag aus den Sagen und Erzählungen der Nakanai, Neupommern, Südsee". *Anthropos*, Vols. 10-11, 1915-16, pp. 34-6, 562-85, 861-87.

A. Kleintitschen: *Die Küstenbewohner der Gazellehalbinsel: ihre Sitten und Gebrauche*, 1906, pp. 1-360.

P. Bley: "Sagen der Baininger auf Neupommern, Südsee". *Anthropos*, Vol. 9, 1914, pp. 196-220, 418-48.

W. J. Read: "A Snake Dance of the Baining". *Oceania*, Vol. 2, No. 2, 1931, pp. 232-37.

G. Bateson: "Further Notes on a Snake Dance of the Baining". *Oceania*, Vol. 2, No. 3, 1932, pp. 334-42.

J. Poole: "Still Further Notes on a Snake Dance of the Baining". *Oceania*, Vol. 13, No. 3, 1943, pp. 224-8.

Carl Laufer: "Rigenmucha, das höchsten Wesen der Baining (Neubritannien)". *Anthropos*, Vols. 41-44, 1946-49, pp. 497-560.

J. A. Todd: "Report on Research Work in S.W. New Britain, Territory of New Guinea". *Oceania*, Vol. 5, No. 1, 1934, pp. 80-101, No. 2, 1934, pp. 193-213.

J. A. Todd: "Native Offences and European Law in S.W. New Britain". *Oceania*, Vol. 5, No. 4, 1935, pp. 437-61.

J. A. Todd: "Redress of Wrongs in S.W. New Britain". *Oceania*, Vol. 6, No. 4, 1936, pp. 401-41.

E. W. P. Chinnery: "Notes on the Natives of Certain Villages of the Mandated Territory of New Guinea". *Anthropological Report* No. 1, 1925, pp. 1-97.

8. BOUGAINVILLE DISTRICT

Passing into the northern Solomon Islands, which are in Australia's Trusteeship, and included in the Kieta Administrative District, we have (with 1940 population figures) Nissan (1,427), Buka (7,608), Bougainville (39,309) and to the north-east the small islands, Carteret (446) Mortlock (178) and Tasman or Nukumanu (99).

Parkinson wrote briefly on these Islands (*Südsee*, pp. 226-272) drawing attention to the Polynesian inhabitants of Mortlock, Nukumanu and of Nuguria (in the New Ireland Administrative Division). K. J. Schaffrath produced *Südseebilder* in 1909, a book of photographs of native life in Buka and Bougainville, and in 1914 Ernst Frizzi published a short survey of the culture of Bougainville and Buka, paying special attention to the Nasioi near Kieta.

Intensive research has been done in three places, by the Thurnwalds, Miss Blackwood and Dr. Oliver. Miss Blackwood spent twelve months about Buka Passage, first on the island of Petats near Buka, and then—and mainly—in the village of Kurtachi on the north coast of Bougainville, from which she was able to visit and study other communities. These people of very dark skin had been subject to much contact, and the old culture was passing, but there was no sign of depopulation, although Miss Blackwood thought this might come. Her results are contained principally in *Both Sides of Buka Passage*. In addition, Mr. G. Thomas has contributed a short chapter on the natives of Buka itself.

Buka and the adjacent tiny islands—the Petats—had a population of 7,608 in 1940, who speak two main tongues—Melanesian in type: Petats in the west and Hanahan in the north-east. The people are of two types, those of so-called "red" skin and those of dark skin. Both the plank canoe and outrigger canoe were made, and big stone objects are found, though not used. Big trumpets are also characteristic. There is also a strong Cargo Cult, and as there is trading between Buka and other islands, and a long history of white contact, Buka itself would repay sociological research. This could be under three headings: ethnology, economics (trading associations), and Cargo Cult.

The interior of the north of Bougainville was in Miss Blackwood's day still "uncontrolled" and hostile to white people. There is no information to suggest any special reason for research there.

Passing the full length of Bougainville to its southern end we come to Buin where Dr. R. Thurnwald did research in 1908, and then years later returned to the same region with his wife to restudy it. As a result we have a unique knowledge of this people at two stages of the process of adaptation to change caused by culture-contact. The people he worked with speak a non-Melanesian language, Rugara (or Terei). The reports by Dr. and Mrs. Thurnwald are listed at the end of this section. Dr. G. C. Wheeler added a few notes on the totemism of the region, and the late Dr. W. J. Perry analysed the genealogical tables collected by Thurnwald.

I suggest that research be done again there by a sociologist with a linguistic flair, for Rugara, which is spoken by about 7,000, is very complicated in structure; the point of further research is that understanding which can only be acquired through a grip of the local language. A sound sociological and psychological approach is taken for granted.

This further study is the more needed, if Dr. Capell's suggestion be accepted that Rugara—the Buin language—be made the medium of instruction for southern Bougainville, as seems reasonable in this predominantly "Papuan" language area. The full understanding of a language requires a thorough knowledge of the culture in which it is an interrelated and functioning element.

Finally, to the west of Buin are the five thousand Siwai or Motuna-speaking people—whose non-Melanesian language is also complex. Dr. D. L. Oliver did anthropological research amongst them for sixteen months in 1938-9, and spent some short periods amongst some other groups. This is good work, but so far only studies of some aspects of the culture, chiefly pigs and land-tenure, have appeared; he underestimates earlier work and methods. Let us hope that more of his results will soon be forthcoming.

Only the briefest information is available about the other "tribes" of the Island, of whom, according to Dr. Oliver, there are nine speaking Papuan languages, and eight speaking Melanesian tongues. He spent a month amongst the Sibbe (or Nagovisi), a tribe of some 3,500 on the north of the Siwai. Mr. Chinnery in 1929-30 also visited the Nagovisi, Siwai and Buin, as well as eight Nasio villages near Kieta, and also some of the Baitsi and Banoni, taking a "sociological" census. The Nasioi number about 3,150, and the Baitsi and Banoni, 2,238.

References

R. Parkinson: *Dreissig Jahre in der Südsee*, pp. 226-46, 247-72.

K. J. Schaffrath: *Südseebilder*. Dietrich Reimer (Ernst Vohsen), Berlin, 1909.

Ernst Frizzi: "Ein Beitrag zur Ethnologie von Bougainville und Buka mit spezieller Berücksichtigung der Nasioi". *Baessler Archiv*. Beiheft 6, 1914, pp. 1-56.

B. Blackwood: "Report on Field Work in Buka and Bougainville". *Oceania*, Vol. 2, No. 2, 1931, pp. 199-220.

B. Blackwood: *Both Sides of Buka Passage*, 1935, pp. 1-599.

G. Thomas: "Customs and Beliefs of the Natives of Buka". *Oceania*, Vol. 2, No. 2, 1931, pp. 220-32.

R. Thurnwald: "Reisebericht aus Buin und Kieta". *Zeitschrift für Ethnologie*, Vol. 41, 1909, pp. 512-32.

R. Thurnwald: "Im Bismarck-Archipel und auf den Salomoinseln, 1906-1909". *Zeitschrift für Ethnologie*, Vol. 42, 1910, pp. 98-147.

R. Thurnwald: *Forschungen auf den Salomoinseln und dem Bismarck-Archipel*, 1912.

R. Thurnwald: "Pigs and Currency in Buin". *Oceania*, Vol. 5, No. 2, 1934, pp. 119-42.

R. Thurnwald: "Stone Monuments in Buin". *Oceania*, Vol. 5, No. 2, 1934, pp. 214-18.

R. Thurnwald: "Profane Literature in Buin". *Yale University Publications on Anthropology*, No. 8, 1936.

H. Thurnwald: "Woman's Status in Buin Society". *Oceania*, Vol. 5, No. 2, 1934, pp. 142-71.

H. Thurnwald: *Menschen der Südsee*. Charaktere und Schicksale, ermittet bei einer Forschungsreise in Buin auf Bougainville, Salomo-Archipel. Stuttgart, Ferdinand Enke Verlag, 1937, pp. viii, 201.

R. Thurnwald: "Some Traits of Society in Melanesia". *Proceedings of the Fifth Pacific Science Congress*, Canada, 1933, Vol. IV, pp. 2805-14

G. C. Wheeler: "Totemismus in Buin (Süd-Bougainville)". *Zeitschrift für Ethnologie*, Vol. 46, 1914, pp. 41-4.

W. J. Perry: "An Analysis of the genealogical tables collected by Dr. Richard Thurnwald in Buin". *Anthropos*, Vol. 9, 1914, pp. 801-11.

P. O'Reilly: "Description Sommaire d'une Collection d'Objets Ethnographiques de l'Ile de Bougainville". *Annali Lateranensi*, Vol. IV, 1940, pp. 163-98.

E. W. P. Chinnery: "Notes on the Natives of South Bougainville and Mortlocks (Taku)". *Anthropological Report* No. 5, 1929-30, pp. 1-125.

D. L. Oliver: "Studies in the Anthropology of Bougainville, Solomon Islands". *Papers of the Peabody Museum of American Archaeology and Ethnology, Harvard University*, Vol. XXIX, 1949, Papers 1-4.

8

THE BRITISH SOLOMON ISLANDS PROTECTORATE

PASSING south and south-east from Bougainville, we quickly reach the first of that double chain of islands, which extends south-east through four and a half degrees of south latitude and nearly seven of longitude, and which forms the Solomon Islands Protectorate. East of San Cristoval are the Reef, Santa Cruz and Vanikoro, with a few tiny islands like Tikopia degrees further east still, all included in the Protectorate.

Several general books have been written on the peoples of the islands or of some of them. R. H. Codrington's *Melanesians* contains material from Ysabel, San Cristoval, Florida, Ulawa and Santa Cruz. W. H. R. Rivers' *History of Melanesian Society*, Vol. I, has a sketchy chapter on the social structure of several of the islands, and a longer chapter on Tikopia. His information on the latter was obtained almost wholly from a native of Uvea who had spent many years there, but as far as the Rev. W. J. Durrad could check, was reliable. R. Thurnwald's summary of his report on his expedition, *Im Bismarck-Archipel und auf den Salomoinseln*, 1906-1909, may be mentioned here, for it gives information for several of the British Solomon Islands (Choiseul-Bambatana on the west coast, Vella Lavella, Rubiana-New Georgia, Simbo and some others).

Amongst missionary literature, F. Coombe's *Islands of Enchantment*, 1911, gives interesting glimpses of the native life and of mission work on Ysabel, Savo, Guadalcanal, Florida, Malaita, Ulawa and San Cristoval; A. I. Hopkins, *In the Isles of King Solomon*, 1928, generalizes somewhat for the British Solomons, though his own personal knowledge is for Mala, on which the book is based, and A. Penny, *Ten Years in Melanesia*, 1888, is concerned mainly with Gela.

Of the natural scientist types, Carl Ribbe's *Zwei Jahre unter den Kannibalen der Salomo-Inseln*, 1903, gives a picture of the inhabitants of the Shortland Islands and New Georgia about 1894. H. B. Guppy, in *The Solomon Islands and Their Natives*, 1887, describes well the "visible" aspects of social organization and life in the Shortlands and

Choiseul, but throws no light on their magic and religion, nor indeed on some important aspects of the social structure. C. M. Woodford, in *A Naturalist among the Headhunters*, 1890, and in short articles, writes on several of the islands, but mainly on Aola in Guadalcanal, where he spent seven months in 1887; he also gives information about Alu where he worked for two months, and Gadotu, near Florida, where he was for three months. E. Paravicini, *Reisen in den britischen Salomonen*, 1931, may also be included.

Considering the number of islands in the Protectorate, and the long period of continuous European contact, comparatively little anthropological research has been done. Indeed, the most thorough, and certainly the most voluminous in results was carried out on the little island of Tikopia with its Polynesian population of 1,288, isolated far to the south-east of Santa Cruz, by Dr. (now Professor) Firth, in 1928-9. Articles, monographs on religion, a very large book on kinship, *We, The Tikopia*, and a book on Tikopian economy, have made the results available. The people were then stable in numbers and filled with interest in, and zest for, life. At present the population is said to be increasing, and men are going from it for work elsewhere. According to Dr. Lambert (*A Doctor in Paradise*, p. 337), the population increase was an effect of the mission rule that all men must marry, thus reversing the natives' policy of imposing celibacy on the younger male members of a family, and also many other checks, for the purpose of keeping the population consonant with the food supply (*Oceania*, Vol. I, No. 1, p. 107). Thus, the first real change in their economics is taking place. Mission work—the Melanesian Mission—has been in progress for about forty years. In view of the inevitable changes in culture, it is of scientific interest that Dr. Firth is reported to be revisiting the island in 1951.[1]

Another of the few sociological projects in the Protectorate was Dr. Hogbin's work in 1927-28 on Ontong Java in the extreme north, of which the chief report is in his *Law and Order in Polynesia*, 1934. The population, which is also Polynesian, was estimated in 1907 at over 5,000, but in 1928 was under 700, and Dr. Hogbin expected that there would "probably be no natives left after a few more years." Fortunately, however, this has not happened. The Melanesian Mission reported a couple of years ago that the population was increasing.

[1]Dr. Firth returned to Tikopia in 1952 with an assistant, Mr. James Spillius.—A. P. E., November 1952.

It is to be hoped that this atoll will be revisited by a social anthropologist, and the readjustment and rehabilitation of the people studied.

These two projects by trained anthropologists have been amongst "Polynesian outliers", and not amongst the Melanesians proper of the Solomons.

We have a few notes for three other Polynesian outliers, Rennell and Bellona with a population in 1931 of 1,500, and Sikayana with 235.

Dr. C. S. Belshaw, on the basis of field study in the Protectorate, the New Hebrides and New Caledonia, especially in the first, produced his valuable *Island Administration in the South West Pacific*, 1950, and also a thesis on "Economics and Culture-Change" in the same regions, which it is hoped will be published soon. The same author has written a brief study on "The Significance of Modern Cults in Melanesian Development".

I. THE WESTERN SOLOMONS

The Shortland, Fauro and Treasury Islands

Commencing with what are known as the Western Solomons, we have some valuable material for the Shortland, Fauro and Treasury Islands immediately south of Bougainville. Carl Ribbe (*Zwei Jahre*, pp. 27-212) gives a good description of observable customs and material culture, and compares the cultures of neighbouring islands. H. B. Guppy, even earlier, in his *Solomon Islands and Their Natives*, 1887, (pp. 13-191) covers the same groups and also Choiseul. Later, G. C. Wheeler (a trained anthropologist working in association with Rivers and Hocart) did research on Mono (Treasury) and Alu in 1908-9, and has published several articles, principally on the totemism and religion. These smaller islands were the sphere of a conquering people, the Mono, who, according to tradition, came from Roviana in New Georgia; they spread along and conquered the "southern" coasts of Bougainville. The census of 1931 gave the population as 1,301, and it was holding its own. This no doubt includes Treasury Island itself.

As this was a conquering and warlike culture, which was subjected to modification both through administrative and missionary (Roman Catholic) influence, and has had to become peaceful, it would repay research. What interest has been substituted for the old one of war-fare and conquest? Did the loss of the latter have the deleterious effect on the culture and population, which was considered almost inevitable thirty and forty years ago? Attention should be paid to the social structure, for Wheeler published nothing on this.

Only one piece of research has been done on the smaller islands between Treasury and New Georgia, namely at Eddystone by A. M. Hocart in 1908. Its proper name is Mandegusu, the map name of Simbo being the name of one of its four villages. His three main articles deal with Warfare, Medicine and Witchcraft, the Cult of the Dead, and with the Canoe and Fishing. Hocart estimated the popu-lation at 400, but it had suffered a serious decrease in the birth-rate, due, said Rivers (*Essays on Depopulation*, pp. 101-2), to loss of interest and the prohibition of head-hunting.

Vella Lavella

Vella Lavella, with a "Papuan"-speaking population of possibly 2,000, is now a Christian island, from which no Cargo Cult has been reported. This suggests a satisfactory adjustment to change—economic, administrative and spiritual, but a thorough sociological study would be very significant in the case of such a Christianized native people, whose former way of life was trading, and also raiding (principally against Choiseul), who were immigrant conquerors from Roviana, and who sent immigrants on to the Shortlands.

New Georgia

Passing down to New Georgia, we have a brief description of the natives of the Roviana (Rubiana) region by Ribbe, based on a visit there in 1895 (*Zwei Jahre*, pp. 259-303). He put the population at about 700 to 800.

No anthropological survey of New Georgia has been made. Dr. Thurnwald for Rubiana on the north-west and Dr. Capell for the Marovo people on the east of the Island, have recorded a few notes. There are said to be about 3,000 Marovo, and another 2,000 using the language. Only vague figures are given for those speaking Roviana.

Unless some practical problem arises, requiring a special anthropo-logical investigation, we must hope that a missionary will prepare an adequate record of the social structure and culture.

Choiseul

For Choiseul, with 4,051 inhabitants in 1931, we have only a few notes, and for Santa Isabel, with about 5,500 in 1931, we have little, apart from Codrington and Coombe. That little includes valuable material from George Bogesi (*Oceania*, 1948), an educated native of Bugotu, who was for a time a native medical practitioner. He is willing to write more and indeed to do field-work in the northern end of Bugotu and Kia, and some arrangement has been made for this purpose. This is a unique opportunity, and I hope it will not be missed.

The populations on these two islands seem very small for their size, and might well be the subject of historical, geographical and anthropological research.

2. THE CENTRAL SOLOMONS

Passing to the Central Solomons we come to the large population region of the group. Florida (Nggela) with about 5,000 people has not been studied by an anthropologist, though Codrington, Coombe and others have recorded material about it.

Guadalcanal

Some research, however, has been done on Guadalcanal by Dr. Hogbin, who in 1933 spent a few days in an inland settlement in the south-east, and then several months at Longgu, whose people have been much "contacted", on the north-east coast. Indeed, the whole island has long been under control. Many of the men of a past generation had worked in Queensland, and most young men work for a few years on plantations, of which there are several on the Island. The population was given in 1933 as 14,215. During the three years 1936, 1937 and 1938, deaths exceeded births, but this was attributed to an epidemic of influenza. The excess for the three years was 100. The recorded birth rate per thousand showed a decrease from 29·9 in 1936, to 24·7 in 1937 and 24·1 in 1938. The death rate was 30·6 per thousand in 1936, and 27·5 and 27·4 in 1937 and 1938 respectively. The war caused an interruption in vital statistics, but the above figures suggest that a careful record of births, deaths, and infant mortality, as well as total figures by sex and age and status, needs keeping and watching. A census has been recently taken.

The population is unevenly distributed, the hills of the interior being sparsely inhabited, at least these days. Dr. Hogbin was able to gather sufficient information about the whole island to establish the existence of three types of social organization on it, one of these—at Marau Sound on the eastern tip—being semi-patrilineal and similar to that of Malaita.

Dr. Capell suggests that for educational purposes three languages would suffice, apart from Marau Sound. (1) For the north coast, east of Visale, Nggele which has already spread from Florida, with which it shares the one type of social organization. (2) Sura, or another form of the language at present used by the Roman Catholic Mission, would be satisfactory for the western sector, in which a system of four matrilineal clans prevails. And (3) Inakona for the south, east of Cape Hunter, a region with matrilineal clans grouped into moieties. This grouping of dialects coincides with the regions of social organization. Further, the Marau corner has a Malaita language as well as social organization.

Malaita

Malaita is an island of great interest and importance. It has the largest population of any island in Melanesia—40,067 in the 1931 census. The people are independent, determined and intelligent, and have supplied the bulk of the labour for plantations in the Protectorate. They provided the favourite source of labour for the Queensland sugar plantations; "with all their treachery and cruelty, their cannibalism and head-hunting", writes Coombe (p. 266), "the men of Mala are the bravest and strongest in the Solomons."

Finally, since the War they have developed a very strong Cargo Cult type of movement, the "Marching Rule", which is anti-white or at least anti-white control, and which repressive measures, even if apparently successful, will only cause to simmer and eventually to boil over. It is a matter for research how far the roots of such a movement go back in the contact history. Referring to the attempts of the Administration in the first decade of the century to bring the Malaitans under control and to prevent them killing one another, Miss F. Coombe reported (p. 271) in 1911 as follows:

"The Government takes action when a murder is duly reported by sending a man-of-war and shelling a village. Needless to say, the murderer takes care to make good his escape, and those who suffer may be perfectly innocent." Resident native police were about to be organized and more effective justice was hoped for. However, the memory of this type of injustice can persist for a long time. It may be a contributing cause to the present situation—a situation which demands very careful, tactful, but skilled sociological research, followed by very definite experiments in the political and economic, as well as welfare fields.

Dr. Hogbin's main work on Malaita in 1933 at the village of Malu'u in the northern tip resulted in his excellent book, *Experiments in Civilization*, 1939, and also in a number of articles of practical value. He also revisited the area at the end of 1943 to see how the experiment of native councils and courts in North Malaita was working (*Oceania*, June 1944).

The experiment was a worthy one, but the war "interruption" brought to a head the reaction to government, with its necessary element of suppression, and to the repression insisted upon by some missionaries; further, the ferment of world ideas, probably little understood, reached even Malaita. Thus, research and new experiment are required. (See e.g. "Malaita: Un Example de Revendications Indigènes", by P. O'Reilly, in *Missions des Iles*, Sept., Oct., 1948, pp. 149-152; also *British Solomon Islands Annual Report*, 1948, pp. 26-29).

It should be emphasized that sociological research has only been done in one very small area of this large island, and that additional sound knowledge is only available for one other region, the village of Sa'a, representing the 5,000 speakers of Little Mala or Sa'a and also three villages of Ulawa, which is closely connected with Sa'a in language and culture. This knowledge we owe to Dr. W. G. Ivens, missionary, who published *Melanesians of the South-East Solomon Islands*, 1927, and in 1930 *Island Builders of the Pacific* (that is, the people of Mala). This is good descriptive work in the earlier non-functional manner; moreover, his first and main work was an attempt to recapture the past with the help of a few informants. In addition there is the Rev. A. I. Hopkins' *In the Isles of King Solomon*, 1928, which deals mainly with Mala.

Of course, some missionaries, expert in a native language, must have a considerable body of knowledge of the culture, but whether they have a real understanding of native reactions to themselves, and to other white contacts, is another matter. In any case, sociological research has only been done in the one district, and more should be done—and by anthropologists willing to master and work in a native language, as distinct from pidgin, a contact and administrative tongue. Dr. Capell has suggested a type language for each of four geographical regions.

3. THE EASTERN SOLOMONS

San Cristoval

For San Cristoval there are Verguet (an early missionary who gives a good summary of the culture), Codrington, Coombe, and mainly Dr. C. E. Fox, for so many years a missionary on the island. His knowledge of the languages is outstanding, particularly for the Arosi and Bauro, the western and middle sections of the island, but he also writes briefly on Kahua, the eastern section and on some of the nearby islands. His work, *The Threshold of the Pacific*, 1924, is very useful on social organization and as a description of religion and magic. His approach, however, is not sociological, and no study of cultural change is attempted.

Santa Cruz and the Reef Islands

Santa Cruz and the Reef Islands have not been intensively studied; Rivers has a chapter, in which he uses material from Mr. Durrad, and also some collected by Professor W. Joest. This last was also used by F. Graebner. Codrington records a good deal from the group, and Speiser and Coombe have written on it. Hector MacQuarrie, an administrative officer, has published an account of his experiences and observations (*Vouza and the Solomon Islanders*, 1946), especially about individual natives. A few other articles have appeared.

With so many regions in which research is required, there is no urgent need for a recommendation regarding these islands. We must look for the day when administrative officers and missionaries will be trained in the methods and theory of social anthropology, so that they will be able to bring this knowledge to their professional work or research done by themselves, and from time to time to present to the world scientific studies of the people among whom they labour.

Population is approximately 5,000.

References

R. H. Codrington: *The Melanesians: Studies in their Anthropology and Folklore*, 1891, pp. 1-419.
W. H. R. Rivers: *The History of Melanesian Society*, 2 Vols., 1914. Vol. I, pp. 1-400; Vol. II, pp. 1-597.

R. Thurnwald: "Im Bismarck-Archipel und auf den Salomoinseln, 1906-1909". *Zeitschrift für Ethnologie*, Vol. XLII, 1910, pp. 98-147.

A. I. Hopkins: *In the Isles of King Solomon*, 1928, pp. 1-267.

Carl Ribbe: *Zwei Jahre unter den Kannibalen der Salomo-Inseln;* Reiseerlebnisse und Schilderungen von Land und Leuten, 1903, pp. 1-352, with many illustrations.

H. B. Guppy: *The Solomon Islands and Their Natives*, 1887, pp. 1-384.

C. M. Woodford: *A Naturalist among the Headhunters*, 1890, pp. 1-249.

C. M. Woodford: "The Canoes of the Bt. Solomon Islands", *J.R.A.I.*, 1909, pp. 506-17.

C. S. Belshaw, *Island Administration in the South West Pacific* (Royal Institute of International Affairs), 1950, pp. 1-149.

C. S. Belshaw, "The Significance of Modern Cults in Melanesian Development", *The Australian Outlook*, Vol. 4, No. 3, 1950, pp. 116-25.

G. C. Wheeler: "Sketch of the Totemism and Religion of the People of the Islands in the Bougainville Straits (Western Solomon Islands)", *Archiv für Religions Wissenschaft*, Vol. 15, 1912, pp. 24-58; 321-58.

G. C. Wheeler: "A Text in Mono Speech (Bougainville Straits, Western Solomon Islands)". *Anthropos*, Vol. 8, 1913, pp. 738-53.

G. C. Wheeler: "An Account of the Death Rites and Eschatology of the People of the Bougainville Straits (Western Solomon Islands)". *Archiv für Religions Wissenschaft*, Vol. 17, 1914, pp. 64-112.

A. M. Hocart: "The Cult of the Dead in Eddystone of the Solomons". Part I and II. *J.R.A.I.*, Vol. 52, 1922, pp. 71-112; 259-305.

A. M. Hocart: "Medicine and Witchcraft in Eddystone of the Solomons". *J.R.A.I.*, Vol. 55, 1925, pp. 229-70.

A. M. Hocart: "Warfare in Eddystone of the Solomon Islands". *J.R.A.I.*, Vol. 61, 1931, pp. 301-24.

A. M. Hocart: "The Canoe and the Bonito in Eddystone Island". *J.R.A.I.*, Vol. 45, 1935, pp. 97-113.

A. M. Hocart: "Fishing in Eddystone Island". *J.R.A.I.*, Vol. 67, 1937, pp. 33-43.

B. T. Somerville (Lt. R.N.): "Ethnographical Notes in New Georgia, Solomon Islands". *J.A.I. of G.B. and I.*, Vol. 26, 1896-7; pp. 357-412.

A. Capell: "Notes on the Islands of Choiseul and New Georgia, Solomon Islands". *Oceania*, Vol. XIV, No. 1, 1943, pp. 20-30.

S. R. Rooney (Rev.): "Notes on Some Customs and Beliefs of the Natives of Choiseul Is., Solomons Group". *Australian Association for the Advancement of Science*, Sydney, 1911, Vol. XIII, pp. 442-5.

G. Bogesi: "Santa Isabel, Solomon Is." *Oceania*, Vol. XVIII, Nos. 3, 4, 1948, pp. 208-33, 327-58.

L. W. S. Wright (Lt. Com.): "The Vele Magic of the South Solomons". *J.R.A.I.*, Vol. 70, 1940, pp. 203-11.

L. W. S. Wright: "Notes on the Hill People of North-Eastern Guadalcanal". *Oceania*, Vol. XIX, No. 1, 1938, pp. 97-101.

A. Penny: *Ten Years in Melanesia*, 1888, 2nd Edition, pp. 1-232.

H. I. Hogbin: "Sorcery and Administration". *Oceania*, Vol. VI, No. 1, 1935, pp. 1-33.

H. I. Hogbin: "The Hill People of North East Guadalcanal". *Oceania*, Vol. VIII, No. 1, 1937, pp. 62-90.

H. I. Hogbin: "Social Organization of Guadalcanal and Florida, Solomon Islands". *Oceania*, Vol. VIII, No. 4, 1938, pp. 398-403.

H. I. Hogbin: "Social Advancement in Guadalcanal, Solomon Is." *Oceania*, Vol. VIII, No. 3, 1939, pp. 289-306.

H. I. Hogbin: "Native Councils and Native Courts in the Solomon Islands". *Oceania*, Vol. XIV, No. 4, 1944, pp. 257-84.

"Notes and Instructions to Native Administrations". *Oceania*, Vol. XVI, No. 1, 1945, pp. 61-70. Drawn up in 1944. Published by H. I. Hogbin.

H. I. Hogbin: "Culture-Change in the Solomon Islands—Report of Field Work in Guadalcanal and Malaita". *Oceania*, Vol. IV, No. 3, 1934, pp. 233-68.

H. I. Hogbin: "Mana". *Oceania*, Vol. VI, No. 3, 1936, pp. 241-75.

H. I. Hogbin: *Experiments in Civilization*, London, 1939, pp. 1-268.

W. G. Ivens: *Melanesians of the South-East Solomon Islands*, London, 1927, pp. i-xxii, 1-529.

W. G. Ivens: "Flints in the S.E. Solomon Islands". *J.R.A.I.*, Vol. 61, 1931, pp. 421-4.

W. G. Ivens: *Island Builders of the Pacific*, 1930, pp. 1-311.

W. G. Ivens: "Native Stories from Ulawa". *J.R.A.I.*, Vol. 44, 1914, pp. 163-94.

H. S. Harrison: "Flint Tranchets in the Solomon Is. and Elsewhere". *J.R.A.I.*, Vol. 6, 1931, pp. 425-34.

P. Verguet, "Arossi ou San Cristoval et ses habitants", *Revue d'Ethnographie*, Vol. 4, 1885, pp. 193-232.

C. E. Fox: "Social Organization in San Cristoval, Solomon Islands". *J.R.A.I.*, Vol. 49, 1919, pp. 94-179.

C. E. Fox & F. H. Drew: "Beliefs and Tales of San Cristoval, Solomon Islands". Parts I and II. *J.R.A.I.*, Vol. 45, 1915, pp. 131-85 and 229-33.

C. E. Fox: *The Threshold of the Pacific*. An Account of the Social Organization, Magic and Religion of the People of San Cristoval in the Solomon Islands. 1924, pp. 1-379.

Eugen Paravicini: "Uber das Muschelgeld der Sudöstlichen Salomonen". *Anthropos*, Vol. 37-40, 1942-45, pp. 158-73.

F. Graebner: *Völkerkunde der Santa Cruz Inseln. Ethnologie*, 1909, p. 71-84.

F. Speiser: "Völkerkundliches von den Santa-Cruz Inseln (mit Beitragen von W. Forg)". *Ethnologica*, Vol. II, part 2, 1916, pp. 153-213.

F. Speiser: "Die Ornamentik von St. Cruz". *Archiv für Anthropologie*, Vol. 13, 1944, pp. 323-34.

Rev. W. O'Ferrall (trans.): "Native Stories from Santa Cruz and Reef Islands". *J.A.I.*, Vol. 34, 1904, pp. 223-34.

H. G. Beasley and F. L. Jones: "Notes on Red Feather Money from Santa Cruz Group, New Hebrides". *J.R.A.I.*, Vol. 66, 1936, pp. 379-91.

A. T. Pycroft: "Santa Cruz Red Feather Money—Its Manufacture and Use". *Journal of the Polynesian Society*, Vol. XLIV, No. 3, 1935, pp. 173-84.

H. MacQuarrie: *Vouza and the Solomon Islanders*. Angus & Robertson, Sydney-London, 1946, pp. 1-218.

R. Firth: "A Native Voyage to Rennell". *Oceania*, Vol. II, No. 2, 1931, pp. 179-90.

R. Firth: "A Dart Match in Tikopia". *Oceania*, Vol. I, No. 1, 1930, pp. 64-96.

R. Firth: "Totemism in Polynesia". *Oceania*, Vol. I, No. 3, 1930, pp. 291-321; Vol. I, No. 4, pp. 377-98.

R. Firth: "Marriage and the Classificatory System of Relationship". *J.R.A.I.*, Vol. 60, 1930.

R. Firth: "The Meaning of Dreams in Tikopia". E. E. Pritchard (ed.) *Essays Presented to C. G. Seligman*, London, 1934, pp. 63-74.

R. Firth: *We, the Tikopia*, London, 1937, pp. 1-599.

R. Firth: *Primitive Polynesian Economy*, London, 1939, pp. 1-380.

R. Firth: *The Work of the Gods in Tikopia*, (2 Vols.), London, 1940, pp. 1-377.

H. I. Hogbin: "A Note on Rennell Island". *Oceania*, Vol. II, No. 2, 1931, pp. 174-8.

H. I. Hogbin: "Spirits and the Healing of the Sick in Ontong Java". *Oceania*, Vol. I, No. 2, 1930, pp. 146-66.

H. I. Hogbin: "The Social Organization of Ontong Java". *Oceania*, Vol. I, No. 4, 1931, pp. 399-425.

H. I. Hogbin: *Law and Order in Polynesia*, 1934, especially pp. 89-234.

H. I. Hogbin: "Depopulation in Ontong Java". *Journal of the Polynesian Society*, Vol. XXXIX, pp. 43-66.

H. I. Hogbin: "Population of Ontong Java". *Oceania*, Vol. X, No. 2, 1939, p. 236.

9

THE NEW HEBRIDES CONDOMINIUM

CAPTAIN Cook's examination of the New Hebrides group in 1774 provided the first reliable information about its people. Sandalwood trading in the first half of the next century resulted in clashes and atrocities; "recruitment" and blackbirding of the islanders for the Queensland Sugar Plantations was a potent factor of depopulation, and introduced epidemics and diseases caused even greater havoc and decline.

Cook's description aroused missionary interest; the London Missionary Society made its first venture in the group in 1839, when John Williams was killed. Bishop G. A. Selwyn of New Zealand began his Melanesian Missionary journey in 1847-48 and 1849, and made linguistic notes. In 1848, too, Presbyterian missions were begun at Aneityum.

Some missionaries published accounts of their work. These record reactions of the New Hebrides to the white man (missionary or trader), as well as to definite proselytizing activity. This is valuable for a study of culture-contact and may well throw light on the present attitudes of the natives. In some cases, the missionaries provided accounts of native society and culture, superficial on modern standards, yet useful. These were regarded by the writers as pictures of what had passed, for the missions' aim was to change the old way of life, to Christianize and civilize—the wearing of clothes often being regarded as a symbol of success. Amongst these books are:

A. W. Murray, *Missions in Western Polynesia, being Historical Sketches of these Missions from their commencement in* 1839 *to the Present Time*, 1863, which deals mainly with Aneiteum, Tanna, Eromanga and Vate (Sandwich).

G. Turner, *Nineteen Years in Polynesia: Missionary Life, Travels, and Researches in the Islands of the Pacific*, 1861; this gives, in addition to missionary experiences on Tanna, a description (pp. 69-94) of Tannese culture and social organization.

R. H. Codrington, *The Melanesians, Studies in Their Anthropology and Folklore*, 1891, belongs to a later period, being based on knowledge gained from 1867 onwards. This work deals in comparative manner with the Torres, Banks and Northern New Hebrides, as well as the Southern Solomons.

William Gunn, the *Gospel in Futuna*, 1914, belongs to the next thirty years' period, Dr. Gunn having commenced work there in 1883. The first part is concerned with missionary work. In the second part (pp. 173-302) the author gives an observer's account of Futuna culture, and also discusses depopulation in the New Hebrides and the Condominium. To the same period belongs Mgr. V. Douceré's *Notes Ethnologiques sur les Populations Indigènes des Nouvelles-Hébrides*, 1924, a booklet. The author began his missionary labours in the group in 1889.

Books of travel and observation by naval officers and others added little to the sum of knowledge of the New Hebrideans, but did sustain interest in them and in what was happening in their islands in the way of commerce and mission work—of clash and conciliation.

J. E. Erskine's *Journal of a Cruise among the Islands of the Western Pacific, including the Feejees and others inhabited by the Polynesian Negro Races*, 1853, (the cruise taking place in 1849), is particularly interesting from this point of view (especially pp. 299-410) for the southern New Hebrides, the Loyalty Group and New Caledonia.

H. H. Romilly's *The Western Pacific*, 1893, includes information about the New Hebrides and also New Guinea and Papua.

The natural historian had not yet turned his steps towards this "No-man's" group of islands, nor were administrative officers appointed to it until the establishment of the Condominium less than fifty years ago.

Missionaries, therefore, were almost the only source of ethnographical information until the first decade of this century was passed. By this time the phase of anthropological and ethnological expeditions had been ushered in by the Cambridge Expedition to Torres Straits in 1899. One of its members, Dr. W. H. R. Rivers, was attracted to Melanesia: as a result of his first journey there in 1908 on the Melanesian Mission vessel, he published in 1914 his two volume work, *The History of Melanesian Society*. The first volume is ethnographical and includes in its survey the Banks and Torres Islands and the New Hebrides, together with the Solomons and Santa Cruz, and also Fiji. This important work follows, both geographically and in general plan, in the wake of R. H. Codrington, but goes deeper and wider in its investigations, and also ventures firmly into theoretical waters.

This same urge to see Melanesia, or a big section of it, as a whole, and to analyse its culture, took Felix Speiser to the Banks Islands and New Hebrides in 1910-1912. His several publications are an indispensable basis for further field-work in the various islands which he visited. These include: Gaua (in the Banks); South and West Santo (pygmies) and Port Olry; Maevo; Aoba; Malo; Big Nambas (in Northern Malekula); Vao; Pentecost; Ambrym (Port Vato); Fate, and Tanna.

Appropriately, Dr. Speiser contributed an important and factual chapter on the New Hebrides, to *Essays on the Depopulation of Melanesia*, which was edited by Dr. Rivers and published in 1922. This work also dealt with the Solomons, three missionaries and the administrator, C. M. Woodford, writing on the problem there. It aroused much interest, not only because of the attention Rivers drew to the psychological factor in depopulation, but also because he emphasized the interdependence of religion, economics, clubs, chieftainship and other institutions in a people's culture and social life. The corollary was a practical one, the insurance of the interlocking relationship of institutions, both old and modified or introduced.

Lastly, M. Jean Guiart, who is attached to the Institut Français d'Océanie, has been working in the New Hebrides during 1949-50, mainly in Ambrym and Tanna. He is to continue this work, extending it to Malekula and Santo, on a grant made by the Condominium Government, on the recommendation of the Director of the Institut Français d'Océanie and the Research Council of the South Pacific Commission. His aim is to gather documentation on native problems.[1]

Torres and Banks Islands

So far, anthropology in the Condominium region had only been concerned with the general survey of its native culture and with its very serious and widespread problem of depopulation. Only missionaries of long service in one area, like Dr. Gunn or le Père Suas, had any deep personal knowledge of the natives. Moreover, starting from the north, we find that intensive research has not yet been carried out in any of the Torres or Banks Islands.

There is, however, much information about the Banks Islands' culture; Codrington devotes a good deal of space to the group, and

[1]This work has been done. M. Guiart is continuing in the study of similar problems within the French territories.—A. P. E., November 1952.

Rivers gives nearly half his Volume I of his *History of Melanesian Society* to a consecutive account of its social organization, to the Sukwe and Tamate societies, and to some customs; neither obtained his material during field-work in the group, but through a few informants. For the Torres Islands, Rivers has only a discussion of kinship. Speiser visited and gives a brief description of the culture (*Südsee, Urwald, Kannibalen*, pp. 253-274).

The Banks Islands' population was estimated in 1893 at 7,300 by a missionary of thirty years' service, but the population of both groups was halved in the first twenty years of this century (Rivers). In the experience of missionaries it had decreased enormously during the preceding forty years, mainly as a result of introduced diseases and recruiting of both men and women. For example, in 1863, 70 out of a population of 900 died in Mota in a "flu" epidemic. In 1871, the west coast of Vanua Lava was deserted because of an epidemic of dysentery. A missionary writing in 1893 said that many villages on the north and east sides of Santa Maria had almost gone, which in 1867 had large populations.

Referring to this same island, also called Gaua, Harrison (*Savage Civilization*, p. 323) says that the population in 1874 was about 15,000, but mainly through epidemics was reduced to 1,250 in 1918 and 679 in 1935, and was still decreasing.

Ureparapara numbered 169 in 1918 and 150 in 1920 (Rivers), and 230 in 1934. Vanua Lava's figure in 1934 was 252. Mota had decreased from 384 in 1917 to 110 in 1934, but is now increasing; Lenormand gives 230 for its 1949 figure ("Visite aux Iles Bank", *Etudes Mélané-siennes*, No. 4, July 1949, pp. 73-77).

Meralava in 1911 numbered 475, all Christian; 506 in 1918; 467 in 1920, 650 in 1934. Rowa in 1911 numbered 40, all Christian. Motlav, in 1920, numbered 568, having fallen from 697 in 1917 (Rivers); it was 630 in 1934. The present population of the Banks Islands, according to M. Maurice Lenormand, is about 4,000. If correct, this represents a big increase on the 2,202 which is given for 1934 (*Pacific Islands Year Book*).

The Torres Islands population in 1950 was only about 200 (*Pacific Islands Year Book*).

References

R. H. Codrington: *The Melanesians* (Index for Torres Island, Banks, Mota, Motlav, Rowa, Ureparapara, Vanua Lava, Santa Maria, Star Island (Meralava)).

W. H. R. Rivers: *The History of Melanesian Society*, Vol. I, pp. 20-188.

F. Speiser: *Südsee, Urwald, Kannibalen*, pp. 252-74.

Maurice H. Lenormand: "Visite aux Iles Bank". *Etudes Mélanésiennes*, No. 4, July 1949, pp. 73-7.

Florence Coombe: *Islands of Enchantment*: seen through many eyes and recorded by F. Coombe, 1911; pp. 1-216 deal with a visit to and description of the Torres and Banks Islands and their peoples. A popular account only.

T. Harrisson: *Savage Civilization*, 1937, pp. 322-3.

W. H. R. Rivers: (ed.) *Essays on the Depopulation of Melanesia*, 1922; especially p. 85.

In the New Hebrides proper, intensive research has been undertaken, mainly on Malekula and the small islands, while Santo and Ambrym have received some attention. Two anthropologists, J. W. Layard and A. B. Deacon, and two biologists, J. R. Baker and Tom Harrisson, have worked in this area.

Espiritu Santo

J. R. Baker gave a brief description ("Depopulation in Espiritu Santo, New Hebrides", *J.R.A.I.*, Vol. 58, 1928, pp. 279-299) of the Sakau on the peninsula on the east of Big Bay, Santo, where he worked in 1922 and. 1927. He also examined the population problem of the island. T. Harrisson discussed this same matter and also described the Sakau and the people of the south-west and centre. B. Deacon obtained from natives he met at Vila some organized information on the social structure graded system and other matters for the Sakau (Hog Harbour) and for other districts of the island, including its south-west.

The above, together with what Speiser recorded, provided a basis for intensive research. Two main projects are suggested. First: an accurate census is needed for the parts of eastern Santo where Dr. Baker took a census, so that the population trend can be studied. In particular, this would be advisable amongst the Sakau and east Santo generally. It should be associated with a sociological study of the people and their culture, selecting for intensive research two sample communities, one Christian and one pagan. Appraisal could thus be made of the effect on the population of cultural changes and of the factors affecting the birth and survival rates. Dr. J. R. Baker's analysis of the position is so significant, theoretically and practically, that it should be restudied, but with a deeper sociological approach.

In the second place, research should be carried out amongst the pygmoid peoples of west and central Santo. Both Speiser (*Südsee*, pp. 128-135) and Harrisson give some information about them.

SUGGESTIONS FOR RESEARCH PROJECTS   119

Dr. Gunn in 1914 gave the total population for Santo, the largest
island of the group, as only 4,500, and Baker, in 1927, as about
4,090.

References
    J. R. Baker: "Depopulation in Espiritu Santo, New Hebrides". *J.R.A.I.*, Vol. 58,
1928, pp. 279-99.
    J. R. Baker: *Man and Animals in the New Hebrides*, 1929; especially pp. 1-80.
    Tom Harrisson: *Savage Civilization*, 1937; especially pp. 371-94.
    Tom Harrisson: "Living in Espiritu Santo". *Geographical Journal*, Vol. 88, 1936,
pp. 243-61.
    F. Speiser: *Südsee, Urwald, Kannibalen:* Reise-Eindrucke aus den Neuen Hebriden,
1913; describes South Santo as well as the pygmoids in West Santo.
    A. B. Deacon: "Notes on some Islands of the New Hebrides" (Edited by C. H. Wedg-
wood). *J.R.A.I.*, Vol. 59, 1929, pp. 461-95. The information is chiefly from Hog
Harbour (Sakau) and from Tismulun in the South-west.
    R. Steel: *The New Hebrides and Christian Missions*, 1880; Chapters XV-XX, for an
account of early history of contact and missions in northern New Hebrides.

Malo

No intensive work has been done on Malo, the main small island
between Santo and Malekula, but its culture and people are related
on the north to Santo and on the south-east to Malekula. Speiser
visited it and a few notes are given by Layard and Harrisson.

In 1914 the population was between 900 and 1,000 according
to Gunn, and in Speiser's opinion was increasing.

References
    J. W. Layard: "Degree-taking Rites in South West Bay, Malekula". *J.R.A.I.*, Vol.
58, 1928, p. 202.
    J. W. Layard: *Stone Men of Malekula:* Vao (see Index).
    T. Harrisson: "Living in Espiritu Santo". *Geographical Journal*, Vol. 88, 1936, pp.
243-61.
    W. H. R. Rivers (ed.): *Essays on the Depopulation of Melanesia*, 1922. (F. Speiser, a
contributor).

Malekula

Malekula, including the Small Islands just off its north-east coast, is
the best known anthropological area of the New Hebrides, but much
remains to be done. Under the influence of Haddon and Rivers of
Cambridge, J. W. Layard in the north-east and A. B. Deacon in the
south-west have made memorable contributions. Attracted to the
Small Islands by the then current interest in the distribution of megalithic culture and by Speiser's reference to its presence in Vao, Mr.
Layard carried out research mainly in Vao in 1914-1915, and as a result
has produced a monumental and thoroughly scientific book, as well

as several articles, and much more is promised. The population of Vao and of the other main Small Islands was about 400 each. It was still the same in 1935.

Layard in *Stone Men of Malekula* gives a valuable outline of the culture of Malekula and the Small Islands, an intensive analysis and discussion of Vao kinship and social organization, a complete functional description and interpretation of the highly developed ritual life, with special reference to Vao and Atchin, and some references to the main island, and a survey of the "graded society complex" in New Hebrides and the Banks Islands. His articles deal with related beliefs.

T. Harrisson (*Savage Civilization* pp. 17-71) gives a literary and summarized description of the related ritual (the Ni-mangki) for Matanavit of the Small Nambas on the northern mainland. And Dr. S. M. Lambert writes a chapter on *Pig Aristocracy*, a trait closely related to the Secret Society Cult. Mr. Layard uses the earlier material of the Rev. Père A. Landes (*Une tribu tombée de la lune*) and the Rev. Père Jean Godefroy (articles in *Les Missions Catholiques*).

Clearly this northern end of Malekula should be visited by an anthropologist who specializes in both social structure and ritual, for the following purposes:—

(1) To examine the population trend in relation to the passing and retention respectively of the former social structure and graded cult-society in different areas, bearing in mind in Vao, Layard's statement (pp. 746-7) that the "inferior side" of the island has always been the first to adopt new elements of culture, whereas the "superior side" is more conservative and better organized. If this be correct, and if it be correlated with population trends, the significance for civilizing and administrative action should be studied.

(2) Related to this is Harrisson's statement that the Atchinese were in 1935 a signal example of "Europeanized Heathenism", and were increasing in numbers. If this be still true, an intensive anthropological field study of this readjustment would be worth while, and not only for scientific interest; for, in spite of missionary endeavour, it is probable that many native communities will develop along this way either directly, or after a stage of apparent acceptance of Christianity. The factors making for stability and progress need to

be determined, and the extent to which they have retained or adapted social, moral and spiritual ideals and sanctions. According to Layard, the Atchinese intensified their own rites in reaction to contact.

(3) Again, the same anthropologist should study the social structure of Matanavit, for Harrisson gives no account of this, and determine to what extent the ritual life is still functioning amongst the Small Nambas.

(4) As soon as possible, an expedition, anthropological, linguistic and medical, should be sent into the northern interior to work amongst the Big Nambas, whose culture was almost unknown in pre-war years, and also unmodified. Speiser, Layard, Cheesman and Harrisson provide some information.

As a warlike, cannibalistic people living in fortified villages, with chiefs, kava-drinking, a graded cult, and organized homosexuality, who will inevitably be brought under control before long, research is required in the first place to discover the factors through which the cohesion and continuity of such a society are maintained—there was no evidence of depopulation in pre-war years—and secondly, on the basis of such understanding, to suggest how modification of their culture in the direction of civilization can be made without undermining the social structure, or inevitably causing a phase of depopulation.

A beginning will be made in studying some of these problems by Jean Guiart, who plans to begin work on Malekula late in 1950. He will carry out research amongst the Big Nambas in north-western Malekula and also amongst some of the coastal population. The investigation is expected to have a bearing on the breakdown of ancient tradition and on the present process of acculturation.[1]

In the rugged interior of the southern half of Malekula is a distinct pygmoid type of people, the Laus, possibly the remnants of the true aborigines, about whom practically nothing is known. Deacon refers to them as Mavur, and thought they might no longer exist. Quite apart from the effects of the inevitable penetration of non-native culture, it is a scientific duty to study and record their way and principles of life, and also to assist in the task of giving them the opportunity to live on in this modern world.

[1]This work has now been completed.—A.P.E., November, 1952.

As for the south-west of the island, and the same is true of the southern fringe, the very title of Deacon's book, *Malekula: A Vanishing People in the New Hebrides*, implies that he was not describing a living pulsating society and culture, but obtaining for ethnology from surviving remnants records of a broken culture. His work was excellent but discouraging to himself. He concentrated on South West Bay and, for four months, at Lambumbu, up the west coast, which is related in ritual to the former. Deacon provides an all-round study of the society and culture, with special emphasis on the ritual and secret societies. Mr. Layard has also given an account of "Degree-taking Rites in South West Bay, Malekula", (*J.R.A.I.*, Vol. 58, 1928, pp. 139-223), obtained from two informants during a very brief visit to the district in 1915, eleven years before Deacon worked there.

The results of their work are of great ethnological value and also of ethnographical value for any field-worker who seeks to "recover" the culture in the neck of the Island, between Laravat and Bushman's Bay. At Lambumbu, however, in 1926, Deacon found the culture broken up, and most of the population away except between jobs. For the south, Layard's and Deacon's writings provide a background of lost culture for a diminishing people. The Rev. C. E. Stallam, writing in 1946, said that in the Mission villages the position varied from no change to a seven per cent annual decrease, while in the bush villages the rate was higher. So bad is the position, that the people have lost confidence in their ability to persist, and this colours all their social and religious life with disinterest and shallowness.

The rate of masculinity is so high that little hope remains. In any case, the research (and treatment) required is primarily medical and biological, with sociology to reveal any ways in which the will to live might be strengthened.

For the whole Island Dr. Gunn gave the 1914 figure as 12,000. The 1944 figure (*Pacific Islands Year Book*) is 7,000.

References

F. Speiser: *Südsee, Urwald, Kannibalen*, 1913, refers to the Vao and Big Nambas.
G. Sebbelow: "The Social Position of Men and Women among the Natives of East Malekula, New Hebrides". *American Anthropologist*, Vol. 15, No. 2, 1913, pp. 273-80. Information from Rev. F. H. L. Paton.
T. Harrisson: op. cit., pp. 395-424. He lived with a group of Big Nambas.
T. Harrisson: "Living with the People of Malekula". *Geographical Journal*, Vol. 88, 1936, pp. 97-128.
L. E. Cheesman: "The Island of Malekula, New Hebrides". *Geographical Journal*, Vol. 81, 1933, pp. 193-210. Refers briefly to Atchin, Big Nambas, Unua (east coast) and South-west Bay.

S. M. Lambert: *A Doctor in Paradise*, 1941, discusses depopulation in Malekula and Graciosa Bay, pp. 235-43.

T. Watt Leggatt: "Malekula, New Hebrides". *Australian Association for the Advancement of Science*, Vol. IV, 1892, pp. 697-708. Gives notes on various aspects of the culture in Port Sandwich District.

J. W. Layard: *Stone Men of Malekula: Vao*, 1942, pp. i-xvii, 1-816.

J. W. Layard: "Atchin Twenty Years Ago". *Geographical Journal*, Vol. 88, 1936, pp. 342-51. Refers to former depopulation, and the effect of contact on various aspects of the culture.

J. W. Layard: "Malekula: Flying Tricksters, Ghosts, Gods and Epileptics". *J.R.A.I.*, Vol. 60, 1930, pp. 501-24.

J. W. Layard: "Shamanism: An Analysis Based on Comparison with the Flying Tricksters of Malekula". *J.R.A.I.*, Vol. 60, 1930, pp. 525-50.

J. W. Layard: "Degree-taking Rites in South West Bay, Malekula". *J.R.A.I.*, Vol. 58, 1928, pp. 139-223.

A. B. Deacon: *Malekula: A Vanishing People in the New Hebrides*. Edited by C. H. Wedgwood, London, 1934, pp. i-xxxvii, 1-789.

A. B. Deacon: "Geometrical Drawings from Malekula and other Islands of the New Hebrides". Edited by C. H. Wedgwood, with Notes by A. C. Haddon. *J.R.A.I.*, Vol. 44, 1934, pp. 129-77.

J. Guiart: *L'Organisation Sociale et Politique du Nord Malekula*. Published by L'Institut Français d'Océanie, 1952.

Omba (Oba; (A)oba; Lepers Island)

For the islands to the east of Santo and Malekula, our anthropological knowledge is meagre. We have to rely mainly on the brief accounts of Codrington, Speiser and Rivers, together with reports from missionaries. A very useful report is "The People of Aoba, New Hebrides" by the Rev. A. S. Webb, who gives a brief description of the social organization and secret society life of the two tribes of the island, and refers to the nearly extinct pygmies who dwelt in the hill country between these two tribes. The population, decreasing in 1911, was still going down in 1937.

Another missionary, the Rev. J. B. Suas, has also written on the people of Aoba, especially about their beliefs, and in addition Deacon gathered a few notes on Aoba from informants at Vila.

The population in 1919 was about 4,000. Harrisson says of it in 1935 that it thrives and increases, is "civilized and charming", yet still partly heathen. The 1944 figure (*Pacific Islands Year Book*) is 5,000.

References

F. Coombe: *Islands of Enchantment*, 1911, pp. 18-29. Population partly Christian; decreasing; some cannibalism; chiefs.

J. B. Suas: "Mythes et Légendes des Indigènes des Nouvelles-Hébrides (Océanie)", *Anthropos*, Vol. VII, 1912, pp. 33-66, for Lolopuepue, Oba.

J. B. Suas: "Notes ethnographiques sur les indigènes des Nouvelles-Hébrides". *Anthropos*, Vol. IX, 1914, pp. 241-60. On population and culture change in the New Hebrides, pp. 241-9; about death, burial and sorcery in Oba, pp. 760-73.

J. B. Suas: "Tamate (Esprits) ou Tamatologie des Lolopuepue (Oba, Nouvelles-Hébrides)". *Anthropos*, Vol. XVI-XVII, 1921-22, pp. 240-6.

F. Speiser: *Südsee*, pp. 236-48.
W. H. R. Rivers (ed.): *The History of Melanesian Society*, Vol. I, 1914, p. 213.
A. S. Webb: "The People of Aoba, New Hebrides". *Mankind*, Vol. 2, No. 4, 1937, pp. 73-80.
A. B. Deacon: "Notes on Some Islands of the New Hebrides". *J.R.A.I.*, Vol. 59, 1929, pp. 495-8.
T. Harrisson: *Savage Civilization*, p. 209.

Maewo (Aurora)

For this island we have only Codrington's references, Speiser's chapter and a few pages in Coombe. According to the last, the population was decreasing in 1911. The Rev. C. Rawson, writing in 1936, said that the total population of North Maewo in 1930 was 100, and estimated the total for the island at 450. However, Dr. Tully who visited Maewo in 1931 to give injections, said that the figure was nearer 700, there being more people in the centre than the Mission was aware of. Indeed, there was a dialect or language in the centre which was unintelligible to the missionaries, and they were conversant with the dialects of North Maewo, Walurigi (Oba) and North Raga (which is the adopted language of South Maewo).

References

R. H. Codrington: op. cit.
F. Speiser: *Südsee*, pp. 97-107.
F. Coombe: op. cit., pp. 30-40.
C. Rawson: letters to Dr. Capell (1936).

Raga (Pentecost)

For Pentecost, we have in addition to Codrington, Speiser and Rivers, a number of contributions by Rev. Père Elie Tattevin and J. B. Suas, missionaries. The social organization and culture generally differs in the northern and southern parts of the Island, the effect of being peopled from Oba and Ambrym respectively.

The population, decreasing in 1911, was about 4,000 in 1914 (Gunn). At present it is about 5,000 (1944 figures, *Pacific Islands Year Book*).

References

F. Coombe: op. cit. 1911, pp. 3-17. Missionary-traveller's description.
W. H. R. Rivers: *The History of Melanesian Society*, Vol. I, 1914, pp. 189-212, is concerned mainly with the kinship system.
E. Tattevin (Rev.): "Sur les bords de la mer sauvage: Notes ethnologiques sur la tribe des Ponorwol L'île Pentecôte (Nouvelles-Hébrides)". *Revue d'Histoire des Missions*, Vol. 4, No. 1, 1927, pp. 82-97.
E. Tattevin (Rev.): "Organisation sociale du Sud de l'île Pentecôte". *Anthropos*, Vol. 23, 1928, pp. 448-63.

E. Tattevin (Rev.): "Mythes et Légendes du Sud de l'île Pentecôte". *Anthropos*, Vol. 24, 1929, pp. 983-1004; Vol. XXVI, 1931, pp. 489-512, 863-81.

J. B. Suas: "Mythes et légendes des indigènes des Nouvelles-Hébrides". *Anthropos*, Vol. 6, 1911, pp. 901-10, deals with Pentecost and Ambrym.

Ambrym

Passing to Ambrym we have, in addition to the material provided by Codrington, Rivers and Speiser, the excellent analysis by Deacon of the regulation of marriage in the island. Rivers' contribution is in a brief article on "Descent and Ceremonial in Ambrym". Layard also refers a good deal to Ambrym, especially to its kinship, megalithic ritual and graded society, and Parkinson (*Dreissig Jahre in der Südsee*, 1907, p. 644) describes the last-named. There is, further, the work done by M. Jean Guiart, who made a study of the social organization of North Ambrym in 1949, and hopes to return there in 1951.[1] The missionary, J. B. Suas, narrates an important myth from Olal in Ambrym, vouching for its indigenous nature and for that of myths recorded for Pentecost and Omba, by the statement that the Hebrideans he knows have only disdain and scorn for the whites.

Harrisson discusses its population position, giving it for 1935 as 3,153 males and 2,438 females, a total of 5,591 and not decreasing. Dr. Gunn, for 1914, reckoned it as between 6,000 and 7,000. If it is still holding its own or increasing, Ambrym should be considered as a possible area for research into the factors making for, and the principles of, adjustment and stabilization in a process of change caused and accelerated by external contact and pressure.

The special problems suggested for both practical and scientific reasons include: (1) The degree to which the social structure has been modified. (2) The function of the introduced graded society, if it still exists, particularly in relation to the whole contact situation. (3) The functional relationship of Christianity in the culture as a whole; and (4) the role of non-native material objects, including money, and their effect on various aspects of the culture.

The 1944 population figure (*Pacific Islands Year Book*) was 3,000. The Rev. W. Paton, however, missionary in Ambrym for a considerable time, who left there in 1948, considered the population to be stationary during his stay there, and to number about 4,100; of these 1,100 are in the south-east and speak a dialect of Paamese, while the

[1] M. Guiart returned to Ambrym in 1951.—A. P. E., November 1952.

3,000 in the rest of the island speak dialects of the Ambrym language, but no other people use it.

References
W. H. R. Rivers: "Descent and Ceremonial in Ambrym". *J.R.A.I.*, Vol. XLV, 1915, pp. 229-33.
A. B. Deacon: "The Regulation of Marriage in Ambrym". *J.R.A.I.*, Vol. LVII, 1927, pp. 461-517.
A. B. Deacon: "Notes on Some Islands". op. cit., pp. 511-15.
T. Harrisson: *Savage Civilization*, pp. 324-5.
R. Parkinson: *Dreissig Jahre in der Südsee*, 1907.
J. B. Suas: "I Tali Tuei, les hommes d'autrefois ou les premiers Hébridais". *Anthropos*, Vols. 12-13, 1917-18, pp. 201-5. This deals with archaeological material.
J. B. Suas: "Mythes et légendes des Indigènes des Nouvelles-Hébrides". *Anthropos*, Vol. 6, pp. 906-10. For the natives' scorn for the whites see p. 902.
Rev. W. Paton: Letter to Dr. A. Capell, 1950.
J. Guiart: "Société, Rituels et Mythes du Nord Ambrym". *Journal de la Société des Océanistes*, Vol. VII, No. 7, pp. 5-103.

Paama

Proceeding south from Ambrym we have no satisfactory studies of Paauma (Paama) and Lopevi, but the former had a population of 1,700 in 1914 (W. Gunn: *The Gospel in Futuna*, 1914) and according to Speiser had survived the first contact, and was increasing, and still was in 1935 (T. Harrisson: *Savage Civilization*, 1937, p. 263). The Rev. W. Paton, who was a missionary on Ambrym, a few miles away, puts Paama at about 2,000.

References
A. B. Deacon: "Notes on Some Islands of the New Hebrides". *J.R.A.I.*, Vol. LIX, 1929, pp. 506-11. Incomplete notes on kinship and social organization collected at Vila.
R. Steel: *The New Hebrides and Christian Missions*, 1880. Has chapters (X-XIV) on the Central New Hebrides, from Paama to Fate, which give history of contact and of missionary efforts.
Rev. W. Paton: Letter to Dr. A. Capell, 1950.

Epi (Api or Tasiko)

Epi has not been studied, though Deacon obtained in Vila a few notes on its social organization and graded society, and Speiser recorded some observations on his visit there. Missionaries have not written about the culture, which resembles that of Ambrym and Paama.

The population had fallen from over 4,000 (perhaps 6,000) in 1900 to about 4,000 in 1914 (W. Gunn, *The Gospel in Futuna*, 1914); it was still declining in 1922 (W. H. R. Rivers: *Essays*, p. 84) and was down to 1,363 in 1943 (Rev. J. G. Miller of Tangoa). Endemic diseases, for which no real counter-measures were taken and unfortunate relations with Europeans were the chief causes. Further, the very fact of serious depopulation led and leads to social disorganization and cultural apathy. This, in its turn, makes recovery all the harder. Epi, therefore, presents a serious medical, psychological and sociological problem. It, or another island presenting a similar problem, would repay careful analysis and diagnosis of the social condition, to be followed at once by a positive welfare and health policy. The Mission considers it could play an important part in the rehabilitation of Epi, by building up a society around the Church, with "the forward look" which is inherent in Christianity. This should be examined.

References
A. B. Deacon: "Notes", op. cit., pp. 498-506.
W. H. R. Rivers: Essays, p. 84.
A. Capell: "The Stratification of Afterworld Beliefs in the New Hebrides". Folk-Lore, Vol. XLIX, 1938, pp. 64-7.
Rev. J. G. Miller, Presbyterian Mission, Tangoa. Written communication to Dr. A. Capell.

The Shepherd Group

(Tangoa, Tongariki, Puninga, Ewose and Valea to Nguna).
This group with its small population is little known in literature. A Presbyterian Mission was established there in 1879. According to the present missionary, the population has risen steadily since the Kanaka trade ceased, apart from epidemic setbacks in 1938 (203 deaths).

The population of Tangoa, the main island of the group, dropped to nearly 900 in 1903, but rose to 1,530 in 1938, and is again over 1,400, after the fatal epidemic of 1938. Tongariki was near 300 in 1946, and Puninga, 80, in the same year, and both increasing.

In Mr. Miller's opinion, Tangoa has a robust population; moreover, it is remotely situated off the regular shipping trade-route, and economically self-sufficient; in addition, the Tangoans have kept their culture "fairly much in its entirety, save in so far as it has been consciously modified by the Christian Church".

This last point is significant because the founder of the Mission, Mr. O. Midhelson, was not an iconoclast; he was prepared to see much of the native culture not only continue, but be incorporated in the life of the Church. The extent to which this has been done, according to the present missionary's summary, covers a wide area of life and thought. This in itself is a subject of research of practical importance within the general problem of culture-change and cohesion. Any phenomenon which is, or which approaches being, a Christianized native culture should be studied historically and functionally. Sir Hubert Murray expressed the view that Christianity could supply that interest, hope and sanction which was undermined by administrative, economic and other changes consequent on contact. Tangoa is an area where this thesis could be examined.

The other important factors, however—relative isolation from shipping routes and economic self-sufficiency—must be borne in mind, for had these been absent, the missionary policy on Tangoa might not have been effective in preserving the culture. Thus Emae (Mae), to the west of the Shepherds, is on the regular cutter route to Vila, has only a small population, and has become dependent on the traders, "who have always been out of all proportion to the local population". Correlated with these three facts is the loss of "a great deal of its traditional culture" (J. G. Miller: the typed communications referred to below under References). Indeed, its culture is tottering and would be gone, except for the close social and cultural ties with Tangoa.

Further south is Nguna, only ten miles from Fate, with which it is closely connected in language. It has lost much of its cultural heritage. Three factors have contributed to this: the labour traffic and absences of men; proximity to Vila, the main centre of non-native influence; and, very significant, the attitude towards native culture of the first missionary, P. Milne, who served in the area from 1870 for about half a century. This was a negative, uncompromising and dictatorial attitude; in particular, Mr. Milne succeeded in undermining the authority of the native leaders, "chiefs", making it difficult for them, even to-day, to exercise their legitimate authority.

The above facts suggest that a comparative study, both historical and in the field, of the populations and cultures of Tangoa, Emae and Nguna would reveal not only the interrelation of geographical position, economic circumstances and missionary policy, but also their relative potency in the process of change.

In 1880 the Mission reported that the Nguna dialect was understood also in the neighbouring islands and mainland of Efate (Fate), and as far north as the Shepherds and Epi. This would facilitate research.

The population of Nguna in 1880 was about 1,000, of the neighbouring island of Pele about 150 and of Emau "considerable". In 1946 the Presbyterian Mission gave 1,600 as the figure for its Nguna district, which includes not only these three islands but also several others on the north-west of Efate, and the northern and greater "half" of Efate itself. As for Nguna, like Paama and Tangoa, according to Harrisson (p. 262) its present day (1935) population is thriving, unshakeable and increasing.

References

R. Steel: *The New Hebrides and Christian Missions*, 1880, gives many facts about the early history of contact and of missions in these districts. See especially chapters XI-XIV, and p. 480.

The typed communication of the Rev. J. G. Miller of Tangoa, already mentioned, has been of much help.

T. Harrisson: *Savage Civilization*. Population in Tangoa, S. Epi, and Nguna etc. pp. 255-6.

Efate (Sandwich Island)

No research has been done on this, the "capital" island of the New Hebrides. Our early knowledge, which is purely descriptive, of obvious, and often unpleasant customs (war, cannibalism, infanticide) comes from the missionaries.

One of these descriptions, given by Turner, was supplied by a Samoan, Sualo, who had been living amongst the Efatese for perhaps twenty years. With his help, the population in 1845 was reckoned at "12,000, perhaps".

Somewhat later knowledge came from the Rev. D. Macdonald, after twenty years at Havannah Harbour.

Missionary efforts of native teachers on Efate, though begun in about 1845, met with many set-backs and little success until the late "1850's", except on the island of Erekor. The first European missionary was stationed at Erekor in 1864, and during the next ten years, others were settled at Havannah Harbour and Fila (Vila). By this time the sandalwood trade had done its worst, and planters and traders were also settling, especially around Vila. The effect of this contact on the population and culture has not been specifically studied. There were, however, the usual disastrous epidemics, and clashes due to "black-birding".

Efate shared in the general New Hebrides decrease. Gunn (1914) gave the population as 900 to 1,000. Rivers (1922) said the survivors had gone to Eretap, Erekor and other islands. By 1935, however, it was increasing, in spite of high masculinity (T. Harrisson, *Savage Civilization*, p. 267) and the *Pacific Islands Year Book*, 1944, gives the number as 1,700.

The problem, chiefly of theoretical interest, is why Erekor and the

130 SOCIAL ANTHROPOLOGY IN MELANESIA

other small islands were the first to welcome missionary work, though
not always with arms consistently open, and then to be rallying points
of population recovery; while the "mainland" with its apparently big
population disintegrated.

Finally, the Central New Hebrides has its mite to contribute to the
study of Cargo Cults and anti-European movements. This last dates
back forty years to the return of the Kanakas, and local prophets had,
long before the war, predicted that America would free the New
Hebrideans,—a prediction, however, which has been proved patently
false. In the late 1920's in particular, this movement had some influence.
It had Cargo Cult features also. There was a temporary "movement"
of the same kind in 1938.

References
G. Turner: op. cit., 1861, pp. 387-95; 445-55; 497-500.
    A. W. Murray: op. cit., 1863, pp. 218-65.
    R. Steel: op. cit., 1880, pp. 215-40.
    T. Harrisson: op. cit. Many references.
    F. Speiser: *Südsee*. Brief chapter.
    D. Macdonald: "Efate, New Hebrides". *Australian Association for the Advancement of Science*, Vol. IV, 1892, pp. 720-35.
    D. Macdonald: "The Mythology of the Efatese". *ibid.*, Vol. VII, pp. 759-68.

Southern New Hebrides

Anthropological research in this region has been at a minimum.
"Blackbirding", sandalwood trade, introduced diseases, clashes with
Europeans, and alcohol had wrought their inevitable deleterious effect
on the population, and missionaries had unwittingly contributed.
But at least these last strove to bring peace and protection, though in
several islands they themselves had to retreat for a time. The Rev.
G. Turner, after seven months of brave effort in 1842, had to leave
Tanna, but he did give an outline description of the people and their
culture, including their constant wars. Thirty years later, the Rev.
W. Gray gave a very helpful paper on the Tannese. For other islands
in this region, our information of the native peoples in the process
of change and contact with Europeans also comes from missionaries:
Dr. Gunn for Futuna; the Rev. John Inglis and Rev. J. Lawrie for
Aneityum; the Rev. H. A. Robertson for Eromanga; and the Rev.
A. W. Murray for Aneityum and Eramanga (Eromanga) as well as
Tanna.

The only anthropological work is C. B. Humphreys' *The Southern
New Hebrides*, 1926, in which he covers the aspects of Eromangan and

Tannese culture as adequately as possible for broken-down cultures and depopulated areas. For the other islands of the region, Aneityum, Futuna and Aniwa, he relies wholly on written sources.

We should remember that the urge to observe and record primitive peoples' ways of life in any methodical manner, and for scientific purposes, did not arise until the second half of last century was well on its way, under the inspiration of men like Tylor and Morgan following on Prichard, and to be followed by Frazer. By that time the native culture of the Southern New Hebrides was almost gone, with perhaps one exception, Tanna. Unfortunately, Humphreys was only a short time on this island and had to work through an interpreter.

In 1878 Tanna had a population of seven or eight thousand, of whom only 120 attended the Mission Services. Up to about 1,500 men had been away at work at the one time in Fiji and Queensland, and on returning were not kindly disposed to mission work. The population in 1914 was from 6,000 to 7,000; according to Humphreys it was increasing in the early 1920's; at present it is reckoned at 6,500. Moreover, it is building up an interesting reaction culture to its many non-native influences. There are Christians, pagans and neo-pagans, and there has been the "John Frum" Cargo Cult movement. Thus, there is coming into being a "modern" mixed type of society—a new order, with roots well in the past, but with eyes to the future and arms out to grasp the present. Studies of the John Frum movement at Tanna have recently been made by Father Patrick O'Reilly ("Prophétisme aux Nouvelles-Hébrides. Le mouvement John Frum à Tanna". *Le Monde non Chrétien*, Paris. Nouv. Série No. 10, April-June, 1949) and by Jean Guiart ("John Frum Movement in Tanna", *Oceania*, Vol. XXII, No. 3, March, 1952), the latter of whom hopes to return there for further work in 1952.[1]

In these days of ferment in native thought, Tanna is a most suitable place for research, so that real psychological and sociological light might be thrown on the process. Further, Humphreys drew attention to the two main groups on the island, of which one, in the south-west, Kauyamera (Kwamers) with "non-Melanesian language" (Humphreys) was little known. This might yet be studied. Actually the language is aberrant Melanesian, and is difficult phonetically.

It is too late to consider research in the other islands. Eromanga had 7,000 people in 1859, and had been much greater. But epidemics,

[1]M. Guiart returned to Tanna in 1952.—A. P. E. November 1952.

for which the missionaries were blamed, soon caused terrific havoc. The figure was below 1,000 in 1914 and is now about 430.

Aneityum

The population of this island, calculated by the Rev. J. Inglis to have been formerly 10,000 or 12,000, had in the late 1850's only 3,500 and by 1878, 1,279; it is now about 200. Aniwa and Futuna each number about the same, the former having been static since 1874, and the latter having fallen from about 900.

References

G. Turner: *Nineteen Years in Polynesia*, 1861, pp. 1-94.

A. W. Murray: *Missions in Western Polynesia*, 1863, pp. 7-212.

R. Steel: *The New Hebrides and Christian Missions*, 1880, pp. 93-214. For southern New Hebrides.

J. D. Gordon: *The Last Martyrs of Eromanga*, 1863. In 1859, only 7,000 on Eromanga, but G. N. Gordon considered it capable of sustaining at least 50,000 (pp. 134-5). Letters of G. N. Gordon record customs and reactions of natives: pp. 135-158. Reason for killing of G. N. Gordon and his wife was an epidemic of measles, for which they were held responsible.

J. Copeland: "Some Niceties of Expression in the Languages of the New Hebrides". *Australian Association for the Advancement of Science*, Sydney, 1887, Vol. 1, pp. 381-483.

J. Lawrie: "Aneityum, New Hebrides". *Australian Association for the Advancement of Science*, Hobart, 1892, Vol. IV, pp. 708-17.

W. Gray: "Some Notes on the Tannese".*Australian Association for the Advancement of Science*, Hobart, 1892, Vol. IV, pp. 645-80.

S. H. Ray: "Stories from the Southern New Hebrides". *J.R.A.I.*, Vol. 31, 1901, pp. 147-55.

F. Speiser: *Südsee, Urwald, Kannibalen: Reise-Eindrucke aus den Neuen Hebriden*, 1913, pp. 275-84.

W. Gunn: *The Gospel in Futuna*, 1914, pp. 1-308.

C. B. Humphreys: *The Southern New Hebrides:* An Ethnological Record. Cambridge, 1926, pp. i-xvi, 1-214.

T. Harrisson: op. cit., pp. 261-3, and see Index for the various islands.

W. Watt (Rev.): Some Children's Games in Tanna (ed. A. Capell). *Mankind*, Vol. 3, No. 9, pp. 261-4.

Patrick O'Reilly: "Prophétisme aux Nouvelles-Hébrides. Le mouvement John Frum à Tanna". *Le Monde non Chrétien*, Paris, Nouv. Serie No. 10, April-June 1949.

Jean Guiart: "John Frum Movement in Tanna". *Oceania*, Vol. XXII, No. 3, March 1952.

Jean Guiart: "Forerunners of Melanesian Nationalism", *Oceania*, Vol. XXII, No. 2, December 1951, pp. 81-90.

Jean Poirier: "Les Mouvements de Libération Mythique aux Nouvelles-Hébrides". *Journal de la Société des Océanistes*, Paris, Tome V, No. 5, December 1949.

10

NEW CALEDONIA AND THE LOYALTY ISLANDS

THIS region was the scene of much clash with Europeans in the first half of last century. Some indication of this is given in Captain J. E. Erskine's *Journal of a Cruise among the Islands of the Western Pacific* in 1849 (published 1853, pp. 337-409). Missions, however, took up the challenge and endeavoured not only to convert the native peoples, but also to act as a buffer. To missionaries, moreover, we are indebted for much of our knowledge of the sociology of the region. Rev. A. W. Murray, *Missions in Western Polynesia* (1863, pp. 266-356) gives a useful account for New Caledonia, the Isle of Pines, Mare and Lifu, and at the same time summarizes previous contact, including James Cook's visit. The Rev. G. Turner, *Nineteen Years in Polynesia*, 1861, gives shorter references. In 1892, the Rev. S. M. Creagh gave a short paper on the Loyalty Islands to the Science Congress in Hobart. Fr. E. Lambert's *Moeurs et Superstitions des Néo-Calédoniens* appeared in 1900. In 1917 Mr. S. H. Ray published a good ethnographic record of the people and language of Lifu, which had been obtained twenty-five years previously from a missionary there, James Sleigh; three years later, Mrs. E. Hadfield, a missionary of thirty years' experience in the Loyalties, gave a general, but rather superficial, description of native life and custom mainly on Uvea and Lifu; and finally, the veteran missionary Maurice Leenhardt published in 1930 his definitive book, *Notes d'Ethnologie Néo-Calédonienne*, on the culture as a whole.

Amongst non-missionaries, Fritz Sarasin, a natural historian, who worked in the region in 1911-12, described the material culture of the Oubatche and Hienghene districts in the north of New Caledonia, and for Kanala (centre) and Yate in the south; he also visited Mare. H. Nevermann's article on "Lifou (Loyalty Inseln)" was published in 1935. E. Rau, *Institutions et Coutumes Canaques*, 1944, introduces new data, and attempts a legal interpretation of custom; and in the July, 1949, number of *Etudes Mélanésiennes*, there is an article written in 1946 by le médecin-Capitaine Fagot, formerly Resident in the Loyalty islands, on "Relations Familiales et Coutumières" as he observed them there, especially amongst the chiefs.

The same Journal prints papers presented to the Pacific Science Congress in New Zealand, 1949. These deal with native education, administration and native welfare, and demographic problems. Statistics show that from 1906, except for the period 1921-26, the population has been increasing steadily, and in 1946 was 18,559 in the main island, 639 in the Isle of Pines, and 11,769 in the Loyalty Islands. Before 1906 the decrease had been serious, the total number having dropped by nearly 14,000 between 1887 and that date. Apparently too, it had also decreased before 1887, for Turner and Murray estimated in 1859 the populations of Uea, Mare and Lifu alone as about 20,000. At present these three islands are estimated at little over half of that figure.

The most interesting and important problem in the region is provided by the advance in citizenship status of the natives of the main island. This step will be watched with great interest by all concerned with the progress of native peoples. Before long, it will be advisable to have a very careful and intensive sociological study made of the effects of this advance. (See for example, "Le Statut des Indigènes" in *Missions des Iles*, September, October, 1948, pp. 132-4).

References

A. W. Murray: *Missions in Western Polynesia*, 1863, pp. 266-356.

G. Turner (Rev.): *Nineteen Years in Polynesia*, 1861.

S. M. Creagh (Rev.): "Notes on the Loyalty Islands". *Australian Association for the Advancement of Science*, Hobart, 1892, Vol. IV, pp. 680-8.

E. Lambert: *Moeurs et Superstitions des Néo-Calédoniens*, 1900.

S. H. Ray: "The People and Language of Lifu, Loyalty Islands". *J.R.A.I.*, Vol. 47, 1917, pp. 239-322.

Emma Hadfield: *Among the Natives of the Loyalty Group*, 1920, pp. 1-316.

M. Leenhardt: *Notes d'Ethnologie Néo-Calédonienne*, 1930, pp. 1-265.

Fritz Sarasin: *Neu-Caledonien und die Loyalty Inseln; Reise-Erinnerungen eines Naturforschers*, 1917, pp. 1-284.

H. Nevermann: "Lifou (Loyalty Inseln)". *Zeitschrift für Ethnologie*, 1935.

R. H. Compton: "String Figures from New Caledonia and the Loyalty Is.". *J.R.A.I.* Vol. 49, 1919, pp. 204-237.

PART III

PRINCIPLES OF A PLAN OF ANTHROPOLOGICAL
RESEARCH IN MELANESIA, RELATED TO NATIVE
WELFARE AND DEVELOPMENT

REPRESENTATIVE SAMPLING

THE preceding survey shows that we possess only a small amount of really penetrating sociological knowledge of the region, when seen against the background of numbers (reaching possibly two million) and of variety of peoples, languages, habitats and contact-experiences. The obverse is that a tremendous amount of information, or rather of understanding, is needed. This, however, can only be obtained on the basis of scientific research, but clearly the projects are manifold. In the past, a field-worker in this region has selected a particular community for research on the advice of a local official or of a previous field-worker because it was a "nice", suitable or "good" and safe village to work in; or because it presented an interesting institution for study, the possibility of "re-capturing" the indigenous organization and culture, the opportunity of working in a *lingua franca*, such as pidgin-English and of getting useful results in one season's work. Thus, each did what was desirable in his own, or in an adviser's eyes. This was all to the good. Anthropological field-work method was still immature. Moreover, all contributions were important for knowledge and theory, for developing method, and for building up an over-all picture; and this was so, even though, in particular cases, the scope of the field-work may seem to have been very limited by reason of the small size of the community studied—a village or island—and though it could be labelled "just academic". Further, if workers and money were unlimited, this individualistic selection of fields could still go on and, perhaps, would not matter, as long as provision were made for co-ordination in the search for general principles of scientific and practical significance.

Now, however, two important facts must be borne in mind. In the first place the number of workers, and probably also the available finance, are limited. In the second place we are faced in this region with urgent problems of great consequence, concerned with the development of peoples and with social and cultural changes, for the direction and effects of which we must bear the responsibility. There-fore, as the possibilities of research are manifold, it is clear that the selection of projects and indeed their very classification, must be according to an over-all plan. The aim of this is to avoid duplication, to minimize the expenditure of energy on the less significant—that is, less significant in present circumstances—and to ensure co-ordination in the study of similar and of different problems in different sub-regions. These desirable ends could be attained by a consultative, if not directing, anthropological research body, representative of the total region; but a classification of the types of needed projects and a recognition of principles governing fields and methods of research are essential.

With regard to the latter: all field-work in this region, whatever the general class of project, must begin with intensive study of a comparatively small group, a village, group of hamlets, group of homestead gardeners, or "horde" of food-gatherers. For the *purpose of this plan of research*, however, such a group should not be selected because of its peculiar interest, but because it is representative of a large population, perhaps occupying most or all of an administrative sub-district, or even more. The results of the research could then be used in administrative (legal, economic and educational) work over the whole cultural area. Indeed, in the method of field-work recommended in this Report, in his third, if not in his second, period of field-work in his selected area, the research worker should familiarize himself with other parts of the wider area of which "his" group is taken to be representative, and so make sure that it is representative, or else indicate the variations, and thus give a wider picture. Hitherto, administrative officers and missionaries have tended to regard visiting anthropologists' results as applying to a very limited field, for example, a village, and to be of no general use.

Although generalizations cannot be made easily for the total region, I suggest that the projects in social anthropology be correlated, where possible, with the larger linguistic groups, each of these being a cultural group, though in some cases groups speaking different languages may be otherwise similar in culture. I have, therefore, taken account of linguistic groupings in the survey and recommendations. Indeed, this survey should be read in conjunction with Dr. Capell's *Survey of Linguistic Research*, prepared for the South Pacific Commission, and shortly to be published for the Commission by the Oxford University Press.

Linguistics and anthropology should work together both in academic institutions and in the field. On the one hand, meaning is culturally determined; and on the other, a people's sociology and psychology cannnot be satisfactorily studied without a deepening knowledge of the language as an aspect of culture and as a medium of thought. The time has come when field-workers must be well-trained and efficient linguists (though not necessarily phonetic specialists). Pidgin and interpreters and phrase-books of the language will not lead to the understanding which is now needed. This is especially so in the types of projects I have classified as "new" and as "critical", and it would add to the value of the "delayed return" type.

Incidentally, by using and recording the language of the peoples whom they are studying, anthropologists will help to make up the great deficiency of specialist linguistic field-workers.

In this connexion, it is not out of place to refer to the post-war policy of the Department of Anthropology in the University of Sydney, seeing that it has been very closely associated with research in the New Guinea-Melanesia region since its foundation in 1926. It is that Honours graduates, the group from which field-workers come, are given an introductory training in linguistics, which can be built on in the case of those proceeding to the field. A very active section of the Department is devoted, under Dr. Capell (Reader in Oceanic Languages), to linguistic research and teaching and is becoming a co-ordinating centre for linguistic research in the region. In addition to linguistic teaching as part of the courses in Anthropology, the University has just approved of a general course in Linguistics, open to all students, and I have no doubt that the linguistic section in Anthropology will become a separate Department, though I hope always closely related to Anthropology. Such is our objective. Experience has shown that Sydney is the most practical place for such development, not only because of the existence of a strong Department of Anthropology, and of strong modern linguistic (including Oriental) schools, but also because Sydney is the most convenient point for contact with the peoples and workers in the Pacific. They visit Sydney and are at the University in a few minutes. Both time and expense might prevent them going further afield. This applies in particular to natives from the Islands who work on boats visiting Sydney, and are helping us build up a library of linguistic recordings; and to missionaries whose Boards are in Sydney, and who contribute much to linguistic research.

In addition to the need for selecting communities on a representative basis, and to the necessity for working in the native language, there is the matter of time to be spent on each type of project. This and other practical aspects will be referred to in the classification of projects.

CLASSIFICATION OF RESEARCH PROJECTS

RESEARCH projects in the region may be grouped into five types according to communities and conditions.

I. NEW DISTRICTS

The first consists of districts in which no research has been done, and where such research would assist administrations and missions beginning work in them. Administration, education, economic development and mission activity based in early stages on an understanding of the peoples concerned, should make for positive progress, lessen friction and, in particular, prevent the adoption of a "double life" and ambivalent attitude, which sometimes characterizes primitive peoples whom we are apt to regard as well governed. Such peoples seem contented and satisfied with the apparently kind and just behaviour and policies of administration and missions; but within themselves individually and communally, they feel wantonly interfered with, and deprived of the just rewards of their labour—as compared with the "good" things we (missionaries, administrative officers and employers) obtain from and in their country. Consequently, behind the scenes, wherever possible, they practise rites which are part of their own cultural heritage, though frowned upon by us, and resort to magic and myth to maintain an even keel in the rough waters of contact and "invasion"; in addition, this is a background for Cargo Cults, "marching lines", and nativistic movements; indeed, it is the predisposing cause, which only requires the emergence of the right personality, combined with some administrative disturbance, of which the aftermath of a war is a special and acute example. Moreover, mere quiescence, resulting from firm and reasonable methods, does not necessarily mean that the trouble has been resolved. The cause is hard to suppress or eradicate when it has been an aspect of the contact situation since the beginning. The Indonesian and Indian situations can be repeated on a smaller, but no less real, scale amongst peoples of primitive culture; indeed, the repetition must come in this modern world, unless the basis of administration and of the economic use of undeveloped countries differ from what it was in the past.

The first pre-requisite is an understanding, not only of the social and political organization, means of livelihood and ritual, but also of the system of values and attitudes to life's problems, old and new, which are part of a people's cultural heritage, and which become part of the individual's "make-up" during the process of growing up and "education". It is not just a matter of recording and respecting the kinship, local and clan affiliations with regard to marriage, land and property. This might preserve the *status quo*. If, however, our aim is not merely to maintain order in our sense of the term and to use native labour and land, but also to assist native people to adjust themselves to the new world from which they can no longer be insulated, we must get down to their social psychology and sociology proper, and be prepared to respect their attitudes, values, aspirations and reactions. These may seem less tangible than social and economic institutions, but they are no less real and potent. Therefore they must be frankly recognized as fundamental factors in the contact situation. Only in this way can real, as distinct from apparent and misleading, co-operation be gained, and a sound foundation be laid for development either in association with the present administering powers, or independently—standing on their own feet.

To understand the system of attitudes, values, aspirations and social sentiments which characterize any particular community, it is necessary that the sociologist should always study very carefully the means and course of personality development in that community. At what ages, by what persons, by what means, and under what conditions does the individual become inculcated with the traditional way of thinking, feeling and acting, hoping and reacting? What is the process by which he is indoctrinated with the community's culture, and so becomes its bearer? The process, in some aspects, is informal, but it is no less real. On the other hand, it is possibly much more formal and stereotyped than is usually thought.

It is not hard to obtain by questioning and observation an outline and superficial knowledge of fundamental social processes; but only a sound knowledge of the language, of the social structure and the culture, will enable the sociologist to realize the implications of what he sees and is told, including the recording of case histories and dreams.

This part of field-work is required by educators, for our educational policy and methods, if they are to succeed, must take stock of and use as far as possible (or make allowance for) the personality development processes in the community which education is designed to assist.

Moreover, if our education method runs counter to this native process and is persevered with, it must educate the individual *out* of his society and make him a misfit, or else cause unnecessary individual and community strain. This, in its turn, might lead to undesirable consequences.

Fortunately, anthropology has been paying much attention in recent years to this side of its work, resulting in an increasing co-operation with psychology. This is particularly so at Sydney.

In doing research in a native community, which is as yet not changed by contact—and indeed even if it is changed—two other practical aspects need to be kept in mind by the social anthropologist. In the first place, what we can call its political and legal system, structure and machinery, must be sought out, analysed in its functional relationship to other aspects of the culture, and highlighted, so that administrative authorities will know the basis on which well-meant political advance should be founded. It is easy to make mistakes in setting up luluais and tultuls[1], or whatever other form of Government control is at first adopted; and it is just as easy to do so in setting up the first forms of local government and courts. If indirect rule be the policy, then effort should be made to see that it *is* working, that is, that rule is through *native* authorities and institutions, as distinct from natives *to whom* authority is given by the external authority. For the latter may lead to friction and disruption.

In the second place, the economic development of the people must be borne in mind. The society, culture, political organization and personality development process will be studied as a functioning whole, but not merely to make a record for history. The economic life of the people must change. But is this change to be only a matter of a third of the able-bodied men being absent to provide labour for non-native concerns, after which they settle back to live off their gardens or, in some parts, by selling copra? If so, we must ask: what does this mean to them in the prime of adult life, and in old age? Have they advanced

---

[1]"Luluai" is a native headman recognized by the Government, who represents the people of his village to the Government. "Tultul" also a local native, is a Government representative.

from the stage of their great grandfathers, except in so far as such customs as we abhor have been suppressed?

The actual results of native wage labour, and of the native copra or coconut producer, must be studied in communities from which the former have come, and in which the latter live. But the possibility of some other method of economic advance *in place of*, or *along with*, wage labour, should be borne in mind by the practical anthropologist in his recommendations with reference to an "undeveloped" community. There may well be environments where there is no alternative. In other places, however, some form of economic community development may be possible, such as peasant farming or co-operative enterprises in production or in some industry. The native land-owning system and methods and customs of co-operation in indigenous activities, would need to be analysed with this possibility in view.

There are still a number of districts, especially in the islands of New Guinea, New Britain and Malekula, of which we have no worthwhile knowledge, and where civilizing activity has hardly begun. These, or a sample of them, should be studied not only for the sake of their own future, but also to throw light on what has happened in other regions where the result of European contact has been unsatisfactory or disastrous, and where remedial measures are required.

The regions selected in this category should be representative samples in the sense emphasized above. Likewise, the work must be intensive and based on the native language and, of course, on residence in the midst of the selected people, as distinct from living at a mission, plantation or official residence. Two years with a three months' vacation after the first eight months should constitute the first session; and this should be followed after a convenient break of about a year for analysing the field material, by at least another year in which the basic system of values and attitudes should be studied. During this period, and also to some extent during his second year in the field, the worker, with his knowledge of the language and social structure, should move around in his total culture area to compare his sample community with others in it, and to get a first hand knowledge of their inter-group attitudes and activities. Ideally too, the same fieldworker should return after a lapse of twelve months or more for, at least, a short period of review. That is about five or six years needs to be devoted to the study of each of the peoples selected in this category. All this may seem a counsel of perfection, but it should be attempted in a few well-chosen areas. Understanding, not description, is needed.

Moreover, since linguistic knowledge is required for its own sake as well as for educational and other aspects of administration and missionary activity, in the first instance, in a completely new field, a linguistic specialist should, if possible, accompany the anthropologist. He could do his basic phonetic, grammatical and vocabulary work while the latter is making his contacts, observing the external forms and activities and studying social structure. His colleague's linguistic results would enable the anthropologist to proceed more rapidly with his own work, and he could, or should be able to, build on them.

The linguist would move on with his mechanical apparatus, phonetics and grammar, leaving the anthropologist to work alone. I doubt whether this is the occasion for teamwork. That would probably be more successful in such new regions, if synchronized with the anthropologist's return for his intensive study of attitudes and values. He would then be in a position to help and advise the other workers in their approach to the natives. The emphasis of the team should, I think, be placed on medical, health, dietary and agricultural research. The anthropologist would then have the task of examining the reactions of the local community during this investigation, and after the team has gone. On the other hand, the presence and activity of a research team in the first couple of years, unless for a fleeting visit, would introduce complicating factors, and lead to doubts, fears and possible non-co-operation of the native people. The basic study of the culture and of values and attitudes is a valuable, if not a necessary, preliminary to such research. The transitory routine visit of an administrative expert is another matter, though he will not get far until understanding is gained.

While the shortage of workers demands a limited and careful selection of "new" districts, there may be a few instances in which research ought to be carried out, even if the numbers concerned be few and their significance in the general scheme seem slight. Thus, no opportunity should be lost to study pygmy groups, and it may still be possible to do so amongst the Tapiro, Pesechem and Mt. Goliath pygmies in Netherlands New Guinea, and those of the Mt. Aiome district in the Trust Territory of New Guinea, and perhaps elsewhere. They are of great interest for sociology and psychology, while for physical anthropology, the relationship of their stature to other factors such as environment, awaits determination. Apart from this, administrations need to know if there be any special difficulties in the process of civilization in the case of pygmies, and if so, how these can be met—a very practical problem for anthropology.

Likewise, an attempt should be made to study a couple of the isolated groups of nomads in the region, both for providing a basis for their stabilization and development, and also to determine the causes and effects of their nomadism. For example, there are the Wakatimi of southern Netherlands New Guinea, and the Heja of the Maramuni River, north of Wabag.

Suggested New Areas and Peoples for Research

Netherlands New Guinea

1. The Baliem in Central Netherlands New Guinea, which is to be controlled.

2. The Middle and Upper Mamberamo, about which little is known.

3. The Wakatimi nomads and the Tapiro pygmies north of them.

4. The Pesechem and Mt. Goliath pygmies.

5. The area north of the Oranje and Sterren Ranges, as soon as penetrated. This field-research might well be done in collaboration with research on the Australian side in the Upper Fly and Telafomin districts.

6. The interior of the "Bird's Head" of which there is no systematic knowledge.

Papua and New Guinea

1. Wabag in the Central Highlands, including the Tari Valley on the Papuan side; for a five-year period of intensive research.

2. The Nembi-Waga Valley in the Central Highlands, Papuan side, which is about to be brought under administration and mission influence.

3. The Kuno, north-west of Chimbu.

4. The Territory of Papua and New Guinea and Netherlands New Guinea central border districts; that is the Upper Fly Waters, Telafomin and the adjacent Netherlands region.

5. The houseless nomadic hunters and sago-eaters of the Rentoul (Papua).

6. The Kukukuku on the Kapau, Upper Tiviri (Lakekamu), the Tauri and Vailala, and further west the Maralinen tribe.

7. An anthropological and census survey of the north-west of the Central Division of Papua (the Upper Kunimaipa and west) to determine numbers, economic development and area for intensive research.

8. The Heja nomads.

9. Anthropological survey across New Britain from Moewehafen to the north coast.

The New Hebrides

1. The Big Nambas of Malekula, who are relatively unknown.

2. Any Pygmy groups.

2. THE DELAYED-RETURN PROJECT

The second type of project is to carry out further research in localities and amongst peoples where sound research on a functional basis was done by trained anthropologists in pre-war years, provided that the community has not practically disappeared. Ideally, this work should be done by the same persons who were in the particular regions previously, for they would have the earlier picture in their minds, publications and notebooks, presumably some familiarity with the language, and also memories of native persons. If they were not available, other workers with a second-hand equipment of this knowledge should be employed.

The object of the research is twofold: first, to compare the present picture of the social organization, economic conditions and religion with the earlier picture, note the changes, if any, and seek the causes and course of that change.

On the academic level this study, pursued in a number of primitive societies which have been in contact with European people and movements, including war, might lead to the establishment of tentative principles of social and cultural change under given conditions. This, however, is obviously also of practical significance; administrations and missions require to know the effect of contact and introduced changes in the various aspects of native life—material, economic, and hygienic—and in the treatment of illness, in magic and belief. If the pre-war studies were sound, and the proposed studies be even better, we will not have to rely on the theory inherent in a functional description and analysis of any given culture and society; that is, we will not simply argue that because of the inter-relationship of this and that (e.g. magic and gardening) or because of the interdependence of this culture trait on that one, alteration of one will lead to alteration of another, and this with another, and so on, perhaps setting up a reverberation or a chain reaction which, if felt throughout the whole culture, might cause its collapse.

In my opinion, this theoretical prediction is correct, but, in itself, of little value. Such reverberations and changes are in process all the time in any culture, being the effects of marriages, deaths, fights, inventions and diffusions of cultural objects and ideas. A culture, however, is elastic and adaptable enough to allow for the re-arrangements involved and also to change customs and adopt new ones. Even objects and some changes in custom arising from contact with such a different culture as our own may be adopted and adapted, and consequent adjustments made successfully so that the society does not suffer damage.

The practical problem is to know what sort of things and what sort of changes, positive and negative, can be introduced without causing disruptions of a people's life and organization, and what are the conditions under which such changes can be successfully made.

The following suggestions, not necessarily new, are worth consideration:

1. The new objects, methods (of gardening, house building, sanitation, burial, treatment of the sick), knowledge (education), moral standards and religious beliefs must be introduced through native authority and acceptance, so that the natives themselves can work out the consequent changes or cultural and social adjustments. They alone can do this, and it takes time, experience and experiment.

Of course, this may seem frustrating to the efficient administrator or zealous missionary, but the development of a people in culture has no meaning apart from their continuing as a people with an integrated social and cultural system. A people cannot be preserved by authority, and no people is willing to be "preserved". A people lives *from within*, or dies out.

Therefore, a few years of patient and understanding presentation of the new objects, customs, rules and beliefs, based on a sound anthropological knowledge of the principles of changes and of attitudes, will reap its reward. The alternative is lack of adjustment, which has a bad effect on individual relationships in the community, or else may cause an apparent adoption of the new ways, together with "the double life" already referred to—the seed of future trouble.

2. In the second place, I suggest that customs which are not old, which are not deeply interwoven with such fundamental institutions as the family and religion, may be changed without any deleterious effects on a people or its culture. To prohibit head-hunting amongst the Trans-Fly tribes, in my opinion a comparatively recent introduction there, might have taken some zest out of life, but it enabled them to live more contentedly.

3. One further suggestion: we must distinguish between changes in culture—that is, in ways of doing, thinking and knowing—which is a process of change, from changes in the social structure, which is a we will not have to rely on the theory inherent in a functional des- basic form of relationships. The kinship, family and clan systems and the local and wider community systems are a structure developed out of the distant past, in which individuals and groups find their places from generation to generation.

The point of this distinction is that modifications of, and changes in, a custom or culture trait do not necessarily affect a people's life and organization adversely, and adjustment to, or adaptation of, the new trait can be made. On the other hand, radical alteration of part of the social structure means a social revolution, affecting the whole. Moreover, it leaves individuals with no place in the structure, or leaves parts of the structure with no individuals in them. Thus a change in the form of the family caused by prohibiting polygyny, or from the joint household to the individual family household caused by a wage system may in the former case leave individuals, that is, some women, with no place in society; or in the latter may cause the break-up of clan or sub-clan solidarity, and leave the single family with no niche or affiliations. Undermining the status of headmen or of hereditary chiefs and even of sorcerers may have the same disintegrating effect. They are important segments or arches in the total structure; once their position is weakened, social cohesion is also weakened. Further, this weakening of the structure can be caused in quite unintentional ways.

For example, the absence of young men, potential fathers, from their villages for an average of five years, working for the European, as was regular in at least one large region before the war, had several repercussions. It tended to make some of them misfits when they returned to what seemed monotonous village life, and to lose respect for the headmen who seemed so backward compared with what they learned in the white man's plantations and mines and on farms; if such attitudes were persisted in, they would cause a weakening of the social structure, that is, of the place of the headmen in it in relation to other men, and the place the members of the village community have in the structure. But whether this occurred or not, the absence of these men for so long meant that they were not being fathers, quite apart from the fact that the women betrothed or married to them frequently made other liaisons. This was an attack on the social structure; the family positions were not being filled in the customary manner, and enough persons not born to maintain the structural positions. For such a people there can be no future. The hasty closing of areas to labour recruiting usually only comes when the disastrous effects are obvious; depopulation has set in, and the structure is falling.

The above are just illustrations of the need to understand a people's social structure, and the effect of all contact and change upon it.

The value then of the delayed-return type of field-work, here advocated, is that we will gain material on which to base laws of change and of culture-contact, with such practical corollaries as I have suggested, but which need examination and testing.

There is a second contribution which these experienced field-workers should set out to make—a presentation and analysis of the native community's system of values, social sentiments and attitudes to other people including ourselves. This is a study which they probably had not made in their earlier work because they were only in the particular field for one period of a year or less, and in any case for not more than two periods—apart from Malinowski in the Trobriands. If, however, they did make such a study, a comparison with the present attitudes and values will be most enlightening, and invaluable for the administrator.

Suggestions for Delayed-Return Projects

' The areas I have in mind, and the anthropologists who have worked in them, are:—

Netherlands New Guinea

Marind-anim	P. Wirz (unlikely to return)
Waropen	Dr. Held

Territory of Papua and New Guinea

Orokaiva	Dr. F. E. Williams (deceased)
Rossel Island	Dr. W. E. Armstrong
Dobu	Dr. R. Fortune
Trobriands	Prof. B. Malinowski (deceased)
Kerema (Orokolo etc.)	Dr. F. E. Williams (deceased)
The Namau (Purari)	,, ,, ,, ,,
Trans-Fly	,, ,, ,, ,,
The Banaro	Prof. Thurnwald
The Abelam (Maprik)	Dr. Phyllis Kaberry
The Arapesh	Dr. Margaret Mead
,, ,,	Dr. R. Fortune
Middle Sepik Communities	Dr. Margaret Mead
,, ,, ,,	Dr. Gregory Bateson
,, ,, ,,	Dr. J. W. M. Whiting
Manam	Miss C. Wedgwood
Admiralty Islands	Dr. Margaret Mead
,, ,,	Dr. R. Fortune
Moewehaven (New Britain)	Mr. J. A. Todd
Lesu (New Ireland)	Dr. Hortense Powdermaker
Tanga	Mr. F. L. S. Bell
Tabar	Mr. W. C. Groves
Buin (Bougainville)	Prof. Thurnwald (unlikely to return)
Buka (Bougainville)	Miss B. Blackwood
Sivai (Bougainville)	Dr. Oliver
Malaita (north)	Dr. H. I. Hogbin
Malaita (south)	Dr. W. G. Ivens (deceased)
San Cristoval	Dr. Fox

The New Hebrides

New Hebrides (northern)	Dr. F. Speiser (deceased)
Malekula	B. Deacon (deceased)
Malekula	J. Layard
New Hebrides (southern)	C. B. Humphreys

A selection would need to be made from these, because of the small number of workers available for the many areas. I suggest, for example: (1) The Maprik area; (2) the middle Sepik; and (3) the Admiralties, because the Japanese were in these areas and because it might be possible to secure the return of at least one of the former experienced workers, Dr. M. Mead for example.

(4) Orokaiva, where there has been much external influence,—missions, plantations and war; where modern ideas are held regarding education and economic development, derived partly through the experience of men in the Papuan Infantry Battalion; and where there are some doubts and dissatisfaction or, at least, misunderstanding of the new economic world they are entering.

(5) Kerema, as a sample from the southern coast of Papua, where the influence of administration and missions has not been modified appreciably by other factors, and where an important ceremonial institution of cohesive function was dying out.

(6) Lesu, as a sample of a community on the mainland of New Ireland which has been in much contact over many years, and to which the former worker could be asked to return.

(7) The northern Solomons. Intensive research should be done in the areas in which Dr. Thurnwald worked on two occasions, separated by twenty-six years, for this would give three stages in the process of change amongst the Buin. The research worker should prepare himself with a thorough knowledge of Dr. and Mrs. Thurnwald's writings in German on the Buin, before beginning this project.

(8) Consideration should be given to the small area in Malaita studied by Dr. Hogbin, provided he or another worker could go to it for a worth-while period, and link it up with a wider study of Malaita, especially in view of the "critical" contact situation there.

(9) Malekula; one or other of the communities studied by Mr. Deacon and Mr. Layard should be restudied.

(10) Tikopia is an example of a small isolated community whose population is increasing and whose young men are now going abroad to work. It will repay re-study by Professor Firth, who, it is understood, will return there in 1951.[1] It is, however, a Polynesian outlier, and possibly not of much significance for the region as a whole. Likewise, the stabilization and readjustment of the population in

[1]Professor Firth returned to Tikopia in 1952.—A. P. E., November 1952.

Ontong Java, another Polynesian outlier, being unexpected, might be studied with profit.

(11) The Trobriand people, on the other hand, are Melanesian, and though not so isolated as the Tikopia, seem not to have suffered a breakdown of either social structure or culture, in spite of the presence of an administrative unit and two missions, a trader, and, during the war, a military hospital. If this view, which was formed on a brief visit there in 1946, is correct, the reasons for the society's stability should be carefully analysed, even though they might seem obvious. A field-worker, as yet inexperienced, went to this island group in 1950.

Note: the plan of obtaining the co-operation of field-workers to return to their pre-war areas in the Australian controlled territories was drawn up in 1946, and forwarded by the Australian National Research Council to the Australian Commonwealth Government, and a reminder later on. Unfortunately nothing was done, possibly because the establishment of the Australian National University and of the Research Council of the South Pacific Commission and the new Australian School of Pacific Administration with its interest in research, raised problems of possible overlap. This means that useful time has gone and also the opportunity of studying attitudes in the important immediate post-war period. (See, too, A. P. Elkin, "Anthropology and the Peoples of the South-West Pacific", *Oceania*, Vol. XIV, No.1, September 1943, pp. 1-19, especially pp. 12-13.)

3. CRITICAL REGIONS

The third type of region to be studied may be termed critical; that is, such communities as have recently passed through, or are passing through, a crisis, the indirect effect of contact. The outward signs of this condition are in some cases depopulation, and in others the so-called Cargo Cults and similar movements. The former is a symptom mainly of direct attack on the social structure, by the withdrawal of native labour from village, social, family and economic life, or by interference with the accustomed diet, possibly caused by this withdrawal, by the introduction of less valuable foods, or by the spread of new diseases, or by all three factors. The search for the causes must be sought, unless the native population has readjusted itself and is no longer declining.

The second symptom, however, is more subtle. It arises from the adaptation which the natives decided they had to make to the European, his demands, ideas and power. But it was not a cultural blending; rather, as previously stated, it was the adoption of a "double life". This was done so well that not even genuine friends of the natives suspected it. Even the "Vailala Madness" and similar happenings elsewhere in pre-war days did not lead to the uncovering of the latent causes and attitudes. It is doubtful, too, whether the native workers' strike in Rabaul in 1920, with its implication of secrecy and organizing power, was really seen for what it was—a symptom of serious attitudes towards the European invader and rule.

It was not till the war that here and there because of changed conditions, natives by their actions and, in some cases later, by their confessions, showed the underlying resentment which ever rankled in their minds against the European. Communist propaganda and Japanese enticements must not be too readily accepted as more than suitable or hopeful occasions for expressing this resentment. The natives who experienced it, lost; but until the causes are analysed, made patent and resolved in a better adjustment, in which the European must play a part, the evil must remain. It may become a repression in the psychological sense, though in many individuals the "double life" will remain a conscious, transmitted attitude and "policy". Cargo Cults are probably symptoms of this condition. It is not satisfactory to attribute these outbursts to the delusions or machinations of an individual or two; nor is it wise to think everything necessary has been done when the community concerned has been apparently convinced of the futility of its delusion or of its guilt. To get things quiet, and watching to quell any fresh signs is, of course, the administrative officer's natural and "correct" approach; but it is not enough. Wise administration will require neither continual repression nor suppression, but understanding of causes and effects, of underlying values and attitudes.

To gain this is a full-time specialist's task. In selected areas where such movements are operating, or quiescent, workers with every sympathy for the administration's function, and equipped with the necessary anthropology, psychology and linguistic ability, should unobtrusively come from the outside, settle, gain the natives' confidence, and work.

If my analysis be anywhere near correct, this research will be most difficult. I am sure, however, that it can be done if the suitable type of person be found. I picture him sincere and quiet, and almost uncon-: sciously inviting the laying bare of the soul, of what goes on unseen, of the struggles and ambivalences in individuals and in groups.

One other proviso: it might be necessary for the district administrative officers to co-operate by being strictly formal with the research-worker, lest the natives form the opinion that the worker is but a spy and informer, instead of a helper. The District Officer, too, must trust the anthropologist not to stir up smouldering fires, while the field-worker, confining himself to observing, listening and objective inquiry, is little likely to do any such thing; indeed, the effect might well be one of catharsis and positive good.

I have drawn attention to this aspect of research, because of my close and responsible association with native administration with its many psychological and sociological difficulties and risks. These are apt to make us fearful of thorough analyses, and to adopt a policy of "letting sleeping dogs lie", and hoping they will not wake up in our time, perhaps never. However, as best world opinion expects administrations to work for native peoples' advance towards self-support and at least association in government, we must base our policies on thorough knowledge of the system of values, attitudes, aspirations and resentments of the peoples for whom we are responsible.

Suggested Critical Regions for Projects

Three types of communities might be selected under this heading: (1) Those in which a Cargo Cult was manifested in pre-war days, but not since. The late Dr. F. E. Williams did this briefly for Vailala (in *Essays Presented to C. G. Seligman*, 1934). Parts of the coast of the northern and north-eastern division of Papua might be included here. Such cults have gone and the Taro Cult is considered by missionaries of long experience to have given rise spontaneously to co-operative farming movements. This needs research.

(2) Those in which an active nativistic outburst apparently followed on the war situation, though its causes might be further back, need study, whether it be mainly religious or political. For example, parts of the north coast of the Trust Territory of New Guinea, such as the Madang coast and hinterland, where the background of contact could be adequately obtained from Maclay onwards, and where the movement has had several important aspects.

(3) Those in which the movement, though recent, is "under control". This may mean dormant and watchful, rather than suppressed. The Biak-Geelvink Bay area of culture-contact and stress and Cargo Cults; the Sepik to Wewak coast, where the Kanaka Cult flourished; Buka; Bougainville; parts of the British Solomon Islands (Malaita in particular), and Tanna.

In all cases special attention should be paid to the apparent human agents through whom the cult arose, or was spread, and the part played by individuals who had held positions of authority or experience in the Administration (Police, Health, et cetera) or had had special opportunity to learn some aspects of the white man's power.

In this category of critical, we could also include such regions as (1) the northern division of Papua, the men of which actively and consciously desire better education, economic possibilities and homes; (2) Manus, where there is a similar urge to become modern; and others where, with or without Cargo Cults, there is a demand for good education.

These urges must be analysed for sources, in relation to the present contact situation and to the native culture and social structure, and for the amount and intensity of active interest. On the basis of this knowledge and of economic possibilities, policy needs to be framed so that progress may be made, and above all, that disillusionment be avoided. Disillusionment leads to "a return to the mat", to nativistic attitudes and to non-co-operation. Such communities become the prey of the demagogue, and provide grounds for those voices of the east which claim to raise the flag of "liberation of all peoples of colour".

Literacy and "Critical" Areas

In these critical areas, I suggest that in addition to giving leading men help and opportunity to understand our system of production, distribution and exchange, and to understand that we rely on work, not our ancestors, for what we possess and distribute, we should press forward hard in our education policies—especially in literacy in an international language such as English. No native lingua franca or pidgin is a satisfactory substitute. Indeed, these are being more and more interpreted by natives as means of keeping something back from them. Resentment, a Cargo Cult and a half-way "return to the mat" will follow. Native peoples must be given access to a world literature, from which they can select what they want (within limitations of catalogues, libraries, income, and availability generally), and not what we decide to translate into the *lingua franca*. This will forestall suspicion and at the same time dissipate ignorance. This does not mean that native languages are to be ignored. Local languages, at any rate those selected on sound regional bases, should be used in the early school years and as the first step in literacy. Moreover, by encouraging literacy in them, pride in, and continuity with, the past is maintained, and also that necessary haven of retreat for "stock-taking", a stage in the culture-change process, is kept intact.

4. CULTURE-CHANGE REGIONS

Related to the "critical" type of projects, is a type which, at present at least, lacks those near-political and other aspects and factors which I have termed critical. It includes projects concerned with culture-change in general and so may be linked with the Delayed-Return type of project. I am thinking here of areas where no previous sociological work was done, or, in some cases, where there is no possibility of the earlier worker returning, and some important practical problem of change has arisen.

For example, in Netherlands New Guinea, research is recommended in the Nimboran tribe where a community development project is being organized; the well-populated Wissel Lakes district where contact processes are operating, and in the Upper Digul country where contact is increasing, where peoples are moving, and where economic development is feasible.

Suggested Culture-Change Areas for Projects

Papua and New Guinea

1.. The Namau where changes are increasing in tempo, and where a community project has arisen spontaneously. There is earlier work (F. E. Williams and J. H. Holmes) from which to start.

2. Manam and the nearby mainland coast, where a study of culture-changes and psychological attitudes would be very useful. Miss Wedgwood, who did one term of research, might return there. Linguistic ability is required.

3. Kainantu (Central Highlands): a study of change under controlled contact, in which all the factors can be known.

4. Nondugl and Hagen: especially for the problem of land-ownership and use, and the effect of the introduction of money.

5. The Baining of New Britain: a comprehensive study of these people is needed concerning their past as well as present condition, and collating all previous data.

6. The Wain and Erap between the South Rawlinson and the head of the Markham: a centre of much economic and war contact.

7. Research into the life and conditions of workers on the goldfields and the effect on life in villages: a woman worker trained in economic and social problems is probably essential.

The British Solomon Islands

1. Shortland and Treasury Islands: a study of the social structure and of the effect of prohibition of war.

2. A sociological study of Vella Lavella—a Christianized native people.

3. Northern Bugotu and Kia: research by George Bogesi, a former native medical practitioner is suggested.

The New Hebrides

1. Northern Malekula, including the Small Islands: based on the earlier work of J. Layard and T. Harrisson.

2. Ambrym.

3. Tangoa, Emae and Nguna: a differential study of culture-contact.

New Caledonia

A sociological study of the widening of citizenship for certain natives.

Mission Anthropologists: In this same context, it is appropriate to indicate where mission anthropologists would be of great value. The list is not exhaustive.

1. The west central division of Papua: Roman Catholic.

2. Islands of the eastern and south-eastern division: Methodist.

3. Morobe district: Lutheran.

I suggest that in all cases, the anthropologist study not only the social, economic and religious effects of the mission, but also the psychological—the attitude to life, culture, joy.

5. BROKEN-DOWN CULTURES AND DEPOPULATION

There is one other category of people or region which opens up a field of useful research; peoples whose culture has broken down, presumably under the stress of contact and clash with Europeans. This includes problems of depopulation and of cultural and social disintegration. These may occur together. The administration's task is to check the former, and, in the latter case, to assist the people to build up a fresh mechanism of cohesion.

The peoples so affected may seem too small to bother about, as in Choiseul. But research in such a community, if intensive enough, might well reveal at this late date causes of disintegration which can then be watched for elsewhere. Moreover, if a people, with or without help, is trying, or is willing, to readjust itself and to develop ways of integration, these should be observed and studied. Likewise, if a people refuses to co-operate with, or is apathetic to, measures taken for its re-establishment, research is clearly indicated into this very fact. In the former case, inquiry may reveal that welfare work and education are required, as Mr. E. W. P. Chinnery reports for the east coast of New Ireland, where he has recently studied the population problem.

Suggested Areas for Projects: Depopulation and Disintegration

Under this heading we may include:

Netherlands New Guinea

A survey of the south-east to study the present social and cultural adjustment, and the population trend.[1]

Papua and New Guinea

1. The Koiari of central Papua: a study in the effect on population of breakdown in social structure.
2. Suau, an unresolved depopulation problem: to be studied along with a nearby people who are increasing, such as the Keveri.
3. The Upper Waria, Biaru and Biangai: a team project, medical, nutritional and anthropological.

[1]Work has begun in the Marind-anim district of Netherlands New Guinea on the South Pacific Commission's project, Population Studies. Dr. H. J. Bijlmer and Dr. S. Kooijman are in charge of investigations.—A. P. E., November 1952.

4. Eastern Sena sub-district: the change in population distribution and in proportion of sexes, with decrease in families. An inquiry by a social anthropologist and a medical expert.

5. Chimbu: an inquiry into the population problem reported by Pastor Bergmann.

6. A woman worker to assist in the study of the population on Fergusson Island.

British Solomon Islands

Choiseul and Ysabel which have small populations for their size.

The New Hebrides

1. Eastern Santo, following on Dr. J. R. Baker's study.

2. Epi.

Conclusion

The foregoing short lists of projects are not exhaustive, but give, in some order of priority in each region and in classes of research, the more important and immediate projects. The survey in Part II gave the background and reasons for the selection, and also information which will help authorities and research institutions to decide on these or on other projects. This list is not meant to imply that there are not many other research projects of great interest, but it is an attempt to present an overall picture of what is needed and would be found useful throughout the total region. The suggested projects should be examined in the light of the survey of earlier information and research, and of the guiding principles suggested in Part III of the Report.

INDEX

Abelam tribe, 87-8, 90, 151
Administration, relation of social anthropology to, 10-12, 16-17, 138, 141-3, 154-5
Administrative officers, duties, 11; need for anthropological training, 12, 14, 16-17, 24, 111
Admiralty Islands, 15, 65, 92, 151-2
Albertis, L. M.d', 26, 35, 37. 47
Ambrym, 118, 124-6, 158
Annali Lateranensi, 8
Anthropologists, on mission staffs, 9-10, 17, 48-9, 69; approach to study of peoples, 13-17, 84-5, 137-40; co-operation between Australian and Dutch, 36-7, 90
Anthropology, descriptive, 13-15, 47; functional, 9, 14-16, 120, 128, 148; delayed return projects, 15-17, 88-90, 138-9, 144-5, 147, 150-3, 157; physical, 24-5; correlation of projects with linguistic groups, 138-9, 145; sampling projects, 137-40
Anthropos, 8-9, 48, 74, 98
Aoba, 123
Arapesh tribe, 87, 151
Archbold Expedition, 33
Armstrong, W. E., 6, 13, 17, 54, 56, 59, 151
Atchinese tribe, 120-1
Aufenanger, *Rev.* H., 79-80
Aufinger, Albert, 9, 71
Austen, Leo, 12, 36, 39-40, 58
Australian National Research Council, 18-19, 64-5, 153
Australian National University, 52, 78, 153
Australian School of Pacific Administration, 153

Baal, J. van, 29
Bainings, 98, 158
Baker, J. R., 5, 118-19, 160
Ballantyne, *Rev.* A., 13, 56
Banaro tribe, 88, 151
Banks Islands, 115-17, 120
Bateson, Gregory, 15, 64, 86, 88, 151
Beaver, W. N., 4, 11, 35, 38, 60, 62
Bell, F. L. S., 64, 94, 151
Bellamy, R. L., 58
Belshaw, C. S., 19, 52, 56, 106
Biak tribe, 28, 33, 156
Biangai tribe, 66, 159
Biaru tribe, 66, 159
Bijlmer, H. J. T., 27, 31-2, 80 *n.*, 159 *n.*
Bina tribe, 38
Blackwood, Beatrice, 15, 101, 151
Blaes, Jacob, 9, 89
Bogesi, George, 108, 158
Bougainville Island, 101-2, 106, 151, 156
British Solomon Islands, research projects, 105-6, 110, 158-60
Bromilow, *Rev.* W. E., 24, 56
Brown, *Rev.* George, 8, 65, 97
Bruijn, J. V. de., 28, 32
Buang tribe, 68
Buin, 16, 102, 151-2
Busama, 16, 19, 67-8

BONIN IS.

Tropic of Cancer

Wake I.

MARIANAS

Saipan ISLANDS

Guam

Yap

Palau

Kwajalein

Ponape

Truk

MARSHALL

CAROLINE

ISLANDS

ISLANDS

Tarawa

GILBERT

Manus

Nauru

Ocean I.

ISLANDS

TERRITORY OF

NEW GUINEA

NETHERLANDS

NEW GUINEA

PAPUA

SOLOMON

ISLANDS

ELLICE

Funafuti

ISLANDS

NORTHERN

Cairns

NEW

HEBRIDES

FIJI

Viti Levu

TERRITORY

ISLAND

NEW

CALEDONIA

AUSTRALIA

Noumea

QUEENSLAND

Brisbane

SOUTH AUSTRALIA

NEW

SOUTH WALES

Norfolk I.

Lord Howe I.

Sydney

Auckland

NEW

VICTORIA

ZEALAND

Welling